THE WORLD OF STATES

D1564734

THE WORLD OF STATES

John L. Campbell and John A. Hall

Bloomsbury Academic
An imprint of Bloomsbury Publishing Plc

B L O O M S B U R Y
LONDON · NEW DELHI · NEW YORK · SYDNEY

Bloomsbury Academic

An imprint of Bloomsbury Publishing Plc

50 Bedford Square
London
WC1B 3DP
UK

1385 Broadway
New York
NY 10018
USA

www.bloomsbury.com

BLOOMSBURY and the Diana logo are trademarks of Bloomsbury Publishing Plc

First published 2015

British Library Cataloguing-in-Publication Data
A catalogue record for this book is available from the British Library.

ISBN: HB: 978-1-8496-6042-6
PB: 978-1-8496-6043-3
ePDF: 978-1-8496-6044-0
ePub: 978-1-7809-3274-3

Library of Congress Cataloging-in-Publication Data
A catalog record for this book is available from the Library of Congress.

Typeset by Integra Software Services Pvt. Ltd.
Printed and bound in India

CONTENTS

Contents

PREFACE

Our collaboration on this book is rather recent despite the fact that we have worked together for many years. John Hall began to write it a few years ago but then set it aside due to other commitments. One of these commitments was a project that he and John Campbell started, thanks to their personal and professional relationships in Denmark. Many years ago, they began to investigate how that small state managed to do so well in a world of increasing political and economic globalization. The former was sure that Danish success stemmed in large measure from its cultural homogeneity and strong sense of national identity. The latter was convinced that it had more to do with the institutional arrangement of its political economy. As it turned out, we were both right. But this led us to wonder how far we could generalize our thoughts to explain the fate of other states. This book is the result.

As readers will quickly see, considerations of national identity and institutional arrangement constitute the principle arc that runs through the entire volume. Our central claim is that we live in a world of states despite the increasing tempo of the global economy. Power is accordingly at the center of our attention, both as it exists within and between states and as it has changed over time. We believe that power has economic, political, and ideological dimensions and insist that it can be either coercive or collective. And we see institutions as the expression of power. Few books have addressed the relationship between nationalism and states in the international political economy, so we view ours as novel in this regard. Herein lie many complexities, and we hope to amuse and to enlighten by highlighting a measure of disagreement between the two of us concerning the extent to which the North, and especially the United States, is losing pre-eminence within the world political economy.

We had particularly productive working sessions in the Vermont Supreme Court's offices, thanks to the generosity of Justice Geoffrey Crawford. At one of these sessions, Geoffrey Crawford, Bill Wohlforth, and Matthew Lange gave us wonderful comments on an early draft of this manuscript. Excellent research assistance was provided by Ignacio Munoz, Qiaoling He, and Ali Zeren. We have received further helpful feedback from Marc Dixon, Susana Borrás, Lev Grindberg, Michael Mann, Francesco Duina, and Ove K. Pedersen. We thank them for their generosity and insight.

This book ends with a series of reflections on the future of states. With that in mind we dedicate it to our grandchildren, to Daniel, Hannah, and Benjamin, and to Ian, Nora, and Alex.

John L. Campbell
Lyme, New Hampshire

John A. Hall
Burlington, Vermont

INTRODUCTION

We live in a world of states—or, if you will, the world in which we live cannot be understood without appreciation of the institutional characters of different types of state and of the nature of the interactions between them. It can be said immediately that this denies outright the claim often made, by politicians as well as by academics, that states are losing their powers as economic interactions around the world increase in speed and intensity. One reason undermining that claim concerns economic and political development, successful still when led by states determined to catch up with the leading edge of power and prosperity. A second reason concerns the advanced core of capitalist society: this is plural rather than singular, run on distinctive lines by differing national political economies. Then there is the European Union (EU). This is not a transnational state but rather an arena in which states meet, regularly and with high levels of civility, so as to iron out differences between them. Finally, much attention will be given in this book to the country that fears to use the very concept of the state. The United States was born from a revolt against an imperial master, with distrust of power politics amplified by war against Germany and Japan—and by cold war competition against the Soviet Union. But instant reflection brings back the reality of the greatest military machine the world has ever known, backed up, we now know, by an astonishingly sophisticated spying apparatus.

We will demonstrate the truth of these statements as we proceed. But there is another way of making readers of this book, most of whom live within the advanced North, instantly aware of the importance of state power—namely, to explain how very much they take for granted what many others so noticeably lack. Such readers live in a world in which states always extract more than a third of gross domestic product (GDP) so as to provide the vast infrastructure—schools, roads, welfare—upon which industrial society depends. But the huge numbers of human beings who live in weak states in Africa and elsewhere have none of this; glancing at their condition can make us realize our own. If we were in their shoes, we would have to protect and defend our own property because courts can barely adjudicate competing claims between neighbors, let alone enforce rulings. Business dealings are often unregulated, so cheating and deceit is common and distrust rampant. Physical security is occasionally left to voluntary militias. The possibility for lawlessness and chaos is sometimes real, especially between ethnic groups vying for supreme power.

This consideration brings us back to the greatest of all theorists of the state, Thomas Hobbes. His experience of civil war led him to insist on the horrid consequences of endless competition between humans:

In such condition there is no place for industry, because the fruit thereof is uncertain: and consequently no culture of the earth; no navigation, nor use of the commodities that may be imported by sea; no commodious building; no instruments of moving and removing such things as require much force; no knowledge of the face of the earth; no account of time; no arts; no letters; no society; and which is worst of all, continual fear, and danger of violent death; and the life of man, solitary, poor, nasty, brutish and short.[1]

That passage is well known. But Hobbes was as clear that in addition to preserving order states needed to fulfill a second task. The world has no single Leviathan: states compete, seeking security in "a perpetual and restless search for power after power." The character of a multipolar world could be detected even in times of peace:

But though there had never been any time wherein particular men were in a condition of war one against another, yet in all times kings and persons of sovereign authority, because of their independency, are in continual jealousies, and in the state and posture of gladiators, having their weapons pointing, and their eyes fixed on one another; that is, their forts, garrisons and guns upon the frontiers of their kingdoms, and continual spies upon their neighbours, which is a posture of war.[2]

The brutal clarity of Hobbes is helpful in understanding states at all times, not least as some of the power of state elites over their societies derives from having to act in the larger geopolitical arena. But his work also helps us understand our world by means of contrast. States have changed since the seventeenth century. The two basic functions at their core—preserving order and security—remain the same, but the means of realizing them are now wholly different.

Two points can be made about the problem of order within states. First, it did not take long for Hobbes's contemporaries to realize that the state he envisaged might itself become a source of disorder, a rapacious entity feeding off its subjects. Accordingly, classical liberal theory sought to control the state, the necessity of whose existence it nonetheless fully recognized. One can encapsulate the change in a neat formula: Hobbes bred John Locke, the theorist of toleration, representation, and the rights of resistance. We add a particular twist to this pair and to the views they represent. Bluntly, allowing voice and accepting compromise is the best means to rule. Inclusion eviscerates radicalism. Accepting the presence of conflict in society ensures political stability insofar as arguments happen all over the place but with few being concentrated on the state. The point deserves underlining. Liberal democracies generate much sound and fury, but most of it signifies little; the conflict in question in part releases steam within systems that are the most stable of modern times. This position is that of liberal Machiavellianism— not an altogether nice position in that it praises liberalism as the best way in which to

---

[1]Hobbes (1982), chap. 13.
[2]Hobbes (1982), chap. 13.

rule.[3] All the same, our addition is necessary and desirable as we can see by emphasizing the distinction between liberalism and democracy. The latter in its pure form can be wholly intolerant, not least on occasions when a single dominant nation that allows no voice at all to minority nationalities is housed within its territory. The institutions that comprise liberalism—rights of assembly, a free press, the inclusion rather than exclusion of minorities—can usefully be seen as putting a limit on majoritarian tyranny.

The second consideration has in fact already been noted but its importance lies at this point. States in the seventeenth century did little for their societies, being in largest part machines for war. The powers of modern states have increased enormously. The huge infrastructure that they create has been noted; just as important is the spread of liberal institutions discussed a moment ago. But one can go further: we now look to our states to stop us smoking and to prevent violence in the most private places of our homes. Leviathans are changing and diversifying, but they are certainly not becoming irrelevant to our daily lives.

The external dimension of state behavior has also changed. One criticism was again directed against Hobbes by his immediate successors. Hobbes had suggested that security could only be found through conquest, through an escalation to extremes. Both Montesquieu and Clausewitz disagreed: total war was unlikely to triumph as it would unite all other states against a potential imperial power. These critics suggested that it was better to seek security through balancing power. That does seem the appropriate lesson to be drawn from European history. But it must be set besides something which is wholly novel. The nuclear revolution has changed just about everything for the advanced states. War is no longer a rational pursuit, the continuation of politics by other means. But this is not for a moment to say that competition between states has ceased to exist. Very much to the contrary, economic competition has gained the centrality once held by the battlefield.

The focus of this book is on the condition of states in this early part of the twenty-first century, on the life chances that result both from living in different types of states and from the interactions between them. One way to understand contemporary circumstances is to look rather more systematically at the past so as illuminate the present by sheer contrast. The sweeping analysis of state formation within Europe's past, which we will present in our first chapter, has led us to one particular general finding that deserves to be highlighted immediately, for it will structure our analysis quite as much as the Hobbesian concerns already mentioned. Whereas Hobbes's generic definition of the state was based on the state's two key functions, the preservation of basic order and protection against other states, we add a third—providing a sense of belonging. This third function allows us to specify the particular character of modern states, especially in comparison to the agrarian empires of the past. What matters in modern circumstances is the imagined community of the nation, which instills a strong sense of belonging among its people.[4]

---

[3]Hall (2013), chapter three.
[4]Anderson (1983).

States were formed in Europe through the crucible of war. There is something to be said, as we shall see, for the view that such high levels of competition were progressive, leading to economic and social development. But by the end of the nineteenth century, a zero-sum situation was reached. There was no more land to conquer, and the remaining great powers found themselves faced with a dilemma. To be powerful meant to be large, but to be large meant that one faced the problem of nationalities within one's domains. Would different nations fight for a larger entity that did not represent them fully? Might they not secede? Would it not be best to become maximally powerful by adding to size cultural homogeneity—that is, to create a nation-state?

The twentieth century witnessed the triumph of the principle of the nation-state. One route to the integration of different nations is that in which states gained power before the emergence of national consciousness. In these circumstances, different nations acceded to a central unitary culture so that eventually each state had its own singular nation, with that nation having the protection of its own state. But we need to remind ourselves that this was not the only means by which nations have been integrated in a state. A second route, illustrated by Switzerland and India, shows that multinational nation-states can and do exist. Rights of all sorts—federal, consociational, and cultural—can give nations sufficient voice that they all become loyal to a large political shell within which they can live.

However, if integration is possible, then so too is the politicization of nation that can lead to secession—that is, to disintegration. Exclusion can intensify nationalist sentiment and precipitate militancy and conflict while inclusion can mollify it. But when states do not allow entry through the granting of rights, nations are often forced to take on the state. What emerges from all of this is an appreciation that nationalism has two sides, as George Bernard Shaw so clearly realized:

> A healthy nation is as unconscious of its nationality as a healthy man of his bones.... But if you break a nation's nationality it will think of nothing else but getting it set again. It will listen to no reformer, to no philosopher, to no preacher, until the demand of the Nationalist is granted.[5]

National solidarity is indeed a source of great strength, though states that possess it often do not realize that their ability to change and to bear burdens rest upon it. But nationalism can also wreak havoc, especially when national difference is linked to class division. Twentieth-century Europe accordingly witnessed the horrors of population transfer, ethnic cleansing, and the Holocaust so that each state might have its own nation and each nation its own state. This was the period in which the great German sociologist Max Weber offered his definition of the state:

> A "ruling organization" shall be called a "*political* organization" if and insofar as its existence and the effectiveness of its order within a specifiable geographical *area*

---

[5]Shaw (1907), pp. xxxiv–xxxv.

are continuously safeguarded by the application and the threat of physical coercion on the part of the administrative staff. A continuously operating compulsory political organization shall be called a "state" if and insofar as it's administrative staff successfully claims the *monopoly* of *legitimate* physical coercion in the implementation of its order.[6]

If one adds to this the concern with cultural uniformity by means of national belonging, one arrives at a world of great late nineteenth-century power containers, seeking to be whole worlds unto themselves. Their conflict led to inter-imperial total wars. What matters for our purpose however is the weakness of the definition. We will show that states in Europe in earlier times had a different character and that the states of our contemporary world are, with one exception, not like that at all.

What, then, is the state? For us, in the most generic and ahistorical terms, the state is a set of institutions designed to maintain order in a given territory and protect its population from other states. But within the modern world, nation-states also strive to instill a sense of belonging and solidarity among those within its borders. The institutions of states typically include decision-making bodies (e.g., councils, senates, parliaments, tribunals), defense and security apparatuses (e.g., armies, navies, militias, national guards), and a set of laws and enforcement mechanisms (e.g., police, councils of elders, judiciary)—all of which are to some extent in the hands of an elite set of rulers and their staff. States may be either constructive and benevolent or predatory and despotic, and some states are better at maintaining order than others. Of course, the institutional composition of states can vary a great deal. We have consciously decided not just to speak about state institutions in the abstract but about their packaging into different countries, given that the interaction between types is a crucial motor of human history.

We will show that some states are stronger than others—a distinction that has consequences for how well they and the societies around them function. By strength and weakness, we refer to two features of the states. One is the capacity of the state to reach into civil society with significant effect. Critical here among other things are the capacities to extract resources through taxation; to maintain peace and control within society; and to facilitate economic development. What we have in mind here is infrastructural power—"the capacity of the state actually to penetrate civil society, and to implement logistically political decisions throughout the realm."[7] This stands in contrast to despotic power, which is the ability of a state to undertake action without any sort of institutionalized negotiations with groups in civil society. Strong states have abundant infrastructural capacities in this regard; weak states have fewer such capacities. By framing things this way, we do not mean to imply a sharp dichotomous distinction between two ideal types of states but rather a continuum ranging from strength to weakness along which one might locate various actually existing states.[8] But another

---

[6]Weber (1980), p. 29. This translation by Scheidel (2013), p. 5.
[7]Mann (1984), pp. 113–114.
[8]For further discussion of this terminology, see Weiss (1998), pp. 28–30.

key feature of state strength or weakness is the presence or absence, respectively, of shared national sentiment among the population. In sum, strong states benefit from well-developed state capacities and shared national sentiment; weak states suffer from underdeveloped state capacities and a lack of shared national sentiment.

Looking ahead

The next chapter looks at the past so as to make it possible, mostly by sheer contrast, to understand our own times. In our view, if states are so important, then we need to know something about where they came from and how they have changed into their present form. The modern nation-state has not been around for very long. We show how states of earlier times differed from the modern state. Previous species of states, but especially the great state powers of the late nineteenth and early twentieth centuries, characteristically thought that they needed extensive territories: military power was believed to rest on population size and economic strength to be guaranteed only by the secure control of raw materials and markets. In this sense, size mattered a great deal. This dependence of the great powers on territory led, in Werner Sombart's terms, to *heroic* rather than to *trading* politics—that is, to inter-imperial conflict rather than commerce; the stakes of conflict were further exacerbated by the nationalities problems that came with the control of large territories. However, size and heroic policies matter much less today. This is thanks in large part to the post–World War II settlement which instituted the principle of non-intervention backed by various security treaties but also thanks to the dramatic rise in international trade, capital flows, migration, and other aspects of what is typically referred to as globalization.

Our second chapter spells out the character of the political economy of the modern world in which today's states operate—and the challenges states must face in this world. In contrast to the previous chapter, which provided a sweeping panorama of the historical evolution of states, this chapter focuses more closely on the novel conditions faced by contemporary states, set against certain continuities that remain from the past. Tensions between the two authors first become apparent in this chapter.

Once this is done, we turn to the varied species of states in the modern world. They rest on a new conceptual language. A mere forty years ago, a brilliant account of modern world politics spoke of the three worlds, that of the West, state socialism, and of the societies seeking to develop so as to catch up—the so-called third world.[9] The world does not look like that now. The division that seems appropriate now is between the global South and the global North—to which we add that of a very special position of the United States, blessed with considerable powers over both.

Chapters 3 and 4 form a pair considering developments in the South. Chapter 3 addresses states often held to be challengers to the current ordering of the world polity.

---

[9]Worsley (1984).

The most celebrated grouping is that of Brazil, Russia, India, and China—the so-called BRICs.[10] We are uneasy with this acronym because Russia is rather different from the rest, not least because it is less a rising power than a great power fallen on hard times. We argue that these countries do not pose as formidable a challenge to the advanced capitalist countries as many have suggested. They want to get in rather than to disrupt.

Chapter 4 begins by considering an altogether different species, the weak states of the global South. Some of these states are so weak that they are unable to maintain order within their borders. Ethnic conflict has broken out in many of them, which has led to much bloodshed—in some cases even genocide—as well as swelling refugee populations. All of this has contributed as well to stunted economic development, thereby exemplifying our view that states that can maintain order, protect their borders, and ensure national solidarity are necessary in order to have a decent society. In prior times, states as weak as this would have been destroyed; the provision of funds from overseas together with the observance of the norm of non-intervention allows them to continue their limited lives. Note that the recent tendency to call such states of the global South "failed" will be resisted here. That terminology is too self-centered, understandable though it is, based on the fear that excessively weak states may cause problems for other states, notably as havens for international terrorists. Of course, weak states do little for their peoples. But to speak of failure misleads by suggesting that these entities could have succeeded. Such empty shells barely had that chance. Still more important is the strong probability that despite their profound weakness, these states are likely to remain with us. Of course, some states have failed absolutely, collapsing in ruins. Where is Burgundy? Where indeed is the Nazi state or the Soviet Union? But few weak states so collapse as to then disappear, most rather remaining in a strange limbo of perpetual half-life. Even Somalia—so often cited as the classic "failed state"—remains in existence. The fact that this is so encourages us to move away from an either/or dichotomy, so as to say a little about the large number of states, from Indonesia to Turkey, and from Chile to Mexico, which do not challenge but which are slowly gaining in powers—that is, those that muddle through in contemporary circumstances.

Chapter 5 turns to the interdependent states of the North. There is tremendous variety within this species of state with each sub-species being organized and coping with the challenges of globalization in different ways. We see little sign of convergence on a single set of common practices. But we make another very general point as well. The balance between the North and the rising powers has not yet been upended in any fundamental way. In other words, Europe, North America, and Japan are still the top dogs in the international political economy and will likely remain so for the foreseeable future. They continue to enjoy sufficient institutional and other capacities that make it likely—although by no means inevitable—that they will adapt successfully to the global challenges confronting them. These capacities are reinforced by a strong sense of national

---

[10]South Africa joined the BRIC countries in 2010. The original four members, however, continue to receive most of the attention, which is why we use this acronym.

solidarity within these states such that nationalism tends be a constructive force in the North whereas it is often destructive in the South. This is an argument, of course, that will not sit well with those who maintain that the rising powers, notably China, will soon overcome the Northern countries economically if not geopolitically or militarily in the years ahead.

The United States, the most formidable power in world history, is the subject of Chapter 6. Much will have been said in earlier chapters about the tremendous international influence of this state both over other countries in the North and over the challengers. Hence the main question that concerns us is whether this can last and what the world would be like if it does not. The future of American hegemony is now hotly debated. The two authors differ most on this issue. But in contrast to those who suspect that America's hegemonic decline will come from external challenges, we do agree that the more serious threat is internal.

Overall, then, this book is about how important states are in today's world—and how important they will continue to be in the future. It is about how territorial size has become less important for the survival and prosperity of states and their societies and how much more crucial their institutional capacities have become for dealing with contemporary challenges, not the least of which is globalization. It is about how nationalism can be an important source of state strength but also a source of tremendous weakness. Finally, it is about the changing balance of power among the leading states of our world.

CHAPTER 1
THE PAST

Prior to the twentieth century, states focused principally on securing their borders and maintaining order within them. Size mattered as territory was deemed essential to secure people, materials, and markets. This precipitated interstate competition as states jockeyed for territorial control. During the nineteenth century, the entry of the people into politics, as workers and nations, meant that states became equally concerned with the issue of belonging. The combination of these factors led to the horrors of the two world wars. Thankfully, this was followed by a postwar settlement whereby national borders were more or less fixed and secured, belonging was established, and order was maintained by various means. This chapter explains how this happened.

Baselines

It is important to begin with a negative. Anthropologists and historians have shown that people seek to escape the coercive powers of a state when they can. This is not simply a question of hunters and foragers being able to manage their lives without state control. Nor is it a question of the peculiarities of bands and chiefdoms such that they cannot properly be called states. More revealing is the ability of nomads to escape the state. A tax gatherer who arrived in the evening at an encampment of Berbers in the High Atlas was liable to find when waking that nobody remained from whom taxes could be taken. This is not to say that stateless societies lack political order: to the contrary, the segmentary principle, pitting a particular layer of one tribe against a similar layer of another, seems to provide stability through a complex balancing mechanism.[1] From these considerations, however, comes a crucial question: if the state is not natural, why was it born?

The best answers involve circumscription, above all being tied down by irrigated land or the cultivation of olives so as to be so caged that escape from the state became difficult. Those who cannot move become fodder for state building.[2] States were invented in this manner on a very few occasions, each based upon a great river valley. In contrast to these few cases of pristine state formation stand the large number of states formed by imitation. It is easy to understand such secondary formation. States have the capacity

---

[1]Gellner (1969).

[2]An alternative theory notes the importance of fear, the need to feed the Gods in the temple that stood at the center of the earliest Mesopotamian state (Crone 1986).

to concentrate power, thereby gaining the capacity to rule over others. Once one state had such force, the only way for people to resist conquest was to get their own. A clear conclusion is apparent: state construction was an evolutionary leap in power, a step from which there was no going back.

Two basic forms of the state dominate the historical record in the agrarian era.[3] The first is the city-state. States of this type developed within power vacuums that allowed them a measure of autonomy. This was true of the city-states of the north of Italy during the Renaissance, and it explains the city-states of West Africa.[4] City-states had particularly intensive social relations, in part because of their characteristically high level of military participation. This in turn was at least sometimes linked to conceptions of democracy—for the few, of course, as in Classical Greece. Finally, city-states often existed within a larger federal world, as was again true of Classical Greece. But the first city-state became an empire, and empires have often been able to co-ordinate resources large enough to absorb a system of city-states, as when Macedon came to dominate the Greek system.[5]

This second basic form of state deserves definition. Empires are like a rimless bicycle wheel: a single center dominates a series of separate communities, bereft of the ability to contact each other.[6] We need to note immediately that this definition is so general as to be capable of encouraging error. Crucially, it does not distinguish between empires of the agrarian and the industrial world. The latter certainly had greater power, although we will see that there is something to be said for the view that imperial power always tends to be exaggerated, as rule is often indirect rather than direct even in modern times. But there can be no doubt about the limits of domination in pre-industrial conditions. It is important to understand why this is so.

The polities in question seem odd to modern eyes. For one thing, elites sat upon a series of rather diverse communities, of varied character in terms of language, religion, and identity.[7] Such communities were laterally insulated from each other. In contrast, the elite had a horizontal identity of its own, shared across space, thereby giving it the power that came from being able to outflank the communities beneath it. These social formations were accordingly not "societies" as we understand that term. The powers of the state were limited, with harsh and arbitrary punishment making up for the inability to provide regularized justice. States were mere "capstones," unable to penetrate deeply into their territories; they were puny leviathans, so bereft of infrastructural reach as to severely curtail their despotic desires, above all through limited capacity to extract taxes.[8] Another way of making the same point is to note the zones of integration of such polities: the outer

---

[3]Trigger (2003).
[4]Burke (1986).
[5]But empires sometimes dissolve in such a way as to allow the re-emergence of city-states, making the pair truly symbiotic.
[6]Motyl (2001).
[7]Gellner (1983).
[8]Mann (1986).

limits depended upon the military, the inner upon genuine market exchange, with tax gathering existing in varied forms between the two—a picture, it can be noted, wholly different from that of our own times.[9] In these circumstances, the daily needs of justice and welfare were often provided through self-help organizations. At best, this could ensure peace through varied mixtures of local and central power; at worst, there might be a power stand-off in which societal power was so limited that the state might succumb to a relatively small challenge—as happened in Rome and on more than one occasion in China when a relatively small number of nomads conquered these large entities.

Another reason why these ancient state forms seem strange to us today is that many authors read back into the past our conception of the nation-state, in which the people have some say, putative or real, over the state in which they live. But it is a terrible mistake, nearly all the time, to imagine that a generally shared sense of belonging existed in the past: states did not benefit from such homogeneity and they lacked sufficient power to create it. It took a long time before such a sense of belonging was achieved even in the advanced parts of the world.[10]

It is just as important not to assume that all states seek to increase their rates of fiscal extraction—a view that is prevalent in certain quarters of social science that presume states to be universally predatory. Indeed, there is at least one major counter-case. In imperial China, rulers sought low rates of taxation in order that the populace would not then be overburdened, so as thereby to remain quiescent.

The final and most obvious point of difference between these former polities and today's of course concerns the monopoly of coercion. Max Weber's definition of the state reflects, as noted, the late nineteenth and early twentieth centuries, an era in which states were seeking to increase their powers. But even then, states did not have a complete monopoly of the forces of coercion. Many officer corps had a measure of autonomy from their states. This lack of sole and legitimate control over coercion is overwhelmingly true for much of the historical record. Sometimes states had the ambition to gain such powers, loathing in early modern Europe the behavior of their "overmighty subjects." But it behooves us to remember that many state leaders in their own time had no conception that a monopoly of coercive power was possible and so did not aim for it. They preferred instead to seek the various compromises with other sections of the elite that allowed them to divide and rule, to balance and thereby to gain a measure of autonomy.

The negative quality of this type of rule in the ancient polities, its concern with balance and stability at the cost of efficiency, derives from the inability to extract large resources from their societies. The maximum surplus available for all purposes in agrarian conditions was never likely to be more than 45 percent of total product.[11] The Roman state—whose powers were relatively great in comparative context given the ease of communication by water—was able to get its hands on perhaps 6 percent of the total product of the empire, mostly spent on the court and the legions, with

---

[9]Lattimore (1962).
[10]Anderson (1983).
[11]Bang (2008).

a much larger share going to the aristocracy, both in Rome and in the provinces. Somewhere between 10 percent and 20 percent of total product was moved around the empire. One striking discovery of the comparative historical analysis of universal empires that follows from this is that all paid systematic attention to the performative aspects of power. Symbols and rituals mattered enormously precisely because of the lack of regularized bureaucracies. Attention was paid to performance precisely because it was so difficult to achieve elite unity.[12] A second noteworthy point stresses that the autonomy of markets was limited. Markets certainly existed but often in order to meet the needs of the state and the demands of the few for luxury goods. Markets lacked autonomy of their own because they were designed instead to serve the polity. There are numerous occasions when politics could interfere with markets, the most celebrated being that of the Chinese state's suddenly curtailing of its successful naval voyages to the East Indies.

Over time, tributary empires tended to move toward something like feudalism as local elites increased their powers at the expense of the center. But this did not necessarily lead to cumulative change. Much more common was the cyclical process that dominated most of human history, in the notion of the Mandate of Heaven or in Ibn Khaldun's wonderful account of Islamic politics, in which weakening at the center was followed by chaos which led in turn to a reunified centralization drive. Karl Marx's contemptuous stress on the lack of real change in the Indian past, on "storm clouds in the political sky" over societies that "vegetated in the teeth of time," captures the general situation nicely.

Modern historiography has made us aware that these great civilizations were successful, for all the rise and fall of dynasties within them. Until something like 1800, their productivity and inventiveness outdid that of Europeans. The logic just described is really that of the American sociologist Talcott Parsons, derided in his day and since for conservatism. But most societies seek to remain true to themselves, disliking change as much as do individuals. The great agrarian civilizations managed to produce sophisticated cultures backed by basic order and prosperity. It is no wonder that so many of these societies lasted so long and no wonder that we marvel today at their achievements.

---

[12]There was great diversity within this general condition. Gellner (1983) offered four contrasts: centralized/ uncentralized, stallions/gelded, open/closed, and fused/nonfused. Each contrast had an illustration: the Papacy compared to the ulamas of Islam, feudal warriors contrasted to the eunuchs so prominent in the Roman and Chinese cases, the meritocratic, examined Mandarinate of China compared to the hereditary Brahmins of the classical Hindu world, and the military orders of Europe pushing expansion to the East seen as so very different from the division of function characteristic of the caste system. These are striking contrasts, but the general picture can be amplified in many ways. For one thing, one needs to remember the tensions that came with conquest. Alexander sought to bring Persian elite into the fold, for instance, but he thereby irritated his Greek companions who feared the loss of privilege and the possibility of being outnumbered and submerged. For another, the ideologies of universalism could vary a great deal. What seems to be most typical is hybridity rather than the imposition of the culture of the center: thus Alexander sought to blend Persians and Greeks through inter-marriage.

The European dynamic

The fundamental point about Europe was that it lacked a similarly coherent civilizational frame: power was held in different hands and a generalized restlessness resulted in endless competition between different polities. A significant part of the explanation for this lies in the splitting of ideological and political power. A "normal" social order, to use the expression of the French sociologist Emile Durkheim, seeks to join power sources together, so that superstructures line up with the baselines of social organization.[13] A typical example is that of the Chinese Mandarinate, offering a creed that supported power, resistant to imagining other social forms even in periods of imperial disunity. The Latin Christian church was very different. Jesus had drawn a distinction between spiritual and worldly power, and this was much exacerbated by St Augustine's *City of God*—which famously insisted, with the memory of imperial persecution at the back of Augustine's mind, that the timetable of God was not the same as that of Rome. In consequence, the church provided the numinous rituals of rule to kings rather than to the empire, thereby doing a great deal to turn Europe in a multipolar direction in which states were forced to compete with each other.

A very simple statistic conveys the result: between 1494 and 1975, European powers were involved in war nearly 75 percent of the time, with perhaps as much as 80 percent of all wars from 1816 to the 1950s being European in origin. In contrast, East Asia saw a three hundred year period of peace between the 1590s and 1894, broken only by barbarian invasions and five fairly small two-state wars.[14] One can add to this the certain fact, testified to by many sources, that fiscal extraction increased enormously over time, as did the military participation ratio, notably in the conscription wars of the twentieth century. We have here endless interaction, between states of course but equally between those states and their own societies, a continual chasing after survival in a threatening world.

But the analytic point about European experience is that it was a failure, unable to create a world that could provide rules and order. But of course change, the move to a new form of some sort, often comes from the margins, from the failures. Europe most certainly changed the world, but it did so because of its status, in comparative perspective, as jejune and juvenile.

The lack of a single center and presence instead of plural and competing ideas and institutions often mandates imitation. There may be something universal here. The sociology of fashion, well understood by Adam Smith and by the French sociologist Pierre Bourdieu, makes much of the status that comes to those at the cutting edge of novelty. In state affairs, the desire to be at such an edge was as present in Voltaire and Montesquieu seeking in the eighteenth century to understand the sources of English success as it was in the United States when researchers in the 1980s sought to understand Japan's economic innovations.

---

[13]Hall (1985).
[14]Mann (2013).

Copying is not always a question of choice but often a matter of survival. The central insight of realism, the theoretical gift given to us by Thucydides, Machiavelli, Hobbes, Rousseau, and Aron, is really that of Darwin: in a world bereft of a single Leviathan states face the "security dilemma," the need to so change themselves as to be able to survive. Necessity is thus the mother of invention. Of course, the functionalism implicit in that phrase hides the obvious fact that many did not adapt and so were absorbed by greater powers. The successful, in contrast, built stronger states. An increase in bureaucracy then allowed for fiscal extraction.

But just as important were vital social changes wrought by multipolar competition. First, defeat by Napoleon at Auerstadt made.a group of reformers aware—instantly— that their own professional armies could no longer compete against a nation in arms, against a force of citizens fighting for their own state. The response to this challenge took less than a decade, with the key component, the abolition of feudalism, being unimaginable without defeat in war. Herein lies the origin of German nationalism. Second, these states came to realize that they had to force economic development so as to gain the industries necessary for military might and geopolitical autonomy. Third, they realized too that progressive social programs were necessary in the face of multipolar geopolitical pressures. The "national efficiency" movement that so affected British politics in first three decades of the twentieth century had its origin in the discovery at the time of the Boer War of the poor health of would-be conscripts—and this point can be generalized given that the extension of welfare benefits often followed major wars, as was true of pensions for veterans and varied rights for mothers at the close of the American civil war. Finally, it is not possible to understand the spread of democracy without reference to participation in war—in all its varied forms, from G.I. bills to votes for women. Endorsement must be given to Trotsky's view that war is the locomotive of history, although that sentiment sits uneasily with its author's commitment to Marxism.

There are two very important corollaries to multipolar competition. The first can be put in the bluntest manner possible. The presence of several states meant that capitalism gained, so to speak, its freedom. The triumph of capitalism owes much to these European conditions. A single image, already noted, makes the point. The Chinese explorations of the fifteenth century were stopped by central state command, probably because resources had to be concentrated so as to deal with a threat coming from the nomads of the North. No equivalent action could be taken in Europe when, for instance, Vienna was threatened by the Turks. Rather, the ability to move around Europe so as to gain patronage is obvious in the case of Columbus, who had tried several states before gaining the patronage of Spain. What is involved can be neatly encapsulated. States had to learn to swim not just in the larger society of state competition but quite as much within the larger sea of capitalist society. There is a complexity here that will be of increasing concern in this book. There can be links between international state and international economic interactions, above all when a truly powerful state can influence the architecture of the world economy.

This leads directly to the second corollary. The notion at its core is that it is dangerous to kill the goose that lays golden eggs. The impact of this second corollary has a variable effect within the historical record, and it is perhaps harder to grasp. As the sinews of the state depend upon money, a measure of decent behavior was recognized as rational by the more intelligent states. An early instance was the *Carta Mercatoria* of 1297: Edward I promised decent treatment and low taxes to merchants if they came to his realm. Many pointed out later that France needed to learn a lesson from the expulsion of the Huguenots in 1685: they moved, and their skills benefited both the United Provinces and England. The variability involved concerns different periods within the history of the economy. The ability to move mattered a great deal in early modern times, and we will argue in later chapters that the ability of capital as well as people to move has enormous import in contemporary circumstances. But imitative late industrialization at the end of the nineteenth and at the start of the twentieth century was slightly different: force then had the capacity, at least for a period, to strengthen economic performance. But the general point is clear, and it contrasts markedly with the situation within pre-industrial empires. Merchants mattered little within the latter, very often being subject to arbitrary confiscations. But to gain power, European kings eventually made alliances with merchants, as Adam Smith noted, and in the process helped create a new world, at first commercial and eventually industrial.

Some words of caution are in order. For one thing, the drive to more unitary and developed states was not so powerful as to rule out alternatives. Interdependent city-states lasted for a long time, and so too did the Hansa, the league of city-states that dominated the Baltics. Furthermore, both pirates and mercenaries retained power for far longer than is generally recognized. More important is a division within the world of states that were built in the early modern period. On the one hand, there is something like an organic quality to development in England and France. An increase in bureaucracy, centralization, and citizenship struggles leading to franchise reform created a national state to begin with and, over time, the basic elements of a modern nation-state. This is a world in which the state as a set of infrastructural and despotic institutions came before national awakenings, thereby allowing a natural process of linguistic homogenization to take place as different ethnic and linguistic groups slowly accommodated to the central state. On the other hand, not all European states resembled this model, and neither, as we shall see, did Great Britain in any complete way. The great empires—Ottoman, Tsarist, and Hapsburg—had arisen out of varied mixtures of conquest and marriage. These social formations were "composite" with key provinces having or gaining "liberties" which the metropole had to respect. Franz Joseph was Kaiser of Austria but King of Hungary, with his realms having no less than fifteen officially recognized languages. States of this type confronted the modern world without the slow organic development of Northwest Europe. The possession of schooling systems lent resilience to nations; state building was thereby bound to be difficult. Bluntly, nations had woken before state construction had been completed. What would become of the idea of the nation-state in these circumstances? Would secession and irredentist politics make it impossible for multinational entities to survive? Let us take up these questions directly.

Europe's Peloponnesian war

An American historian, John Nef, once suggested, with the factors just discussed in mind, that there was a link between war and human progress.[15] It is certainly true that the endless rationalization in societies and states—by which we mean institutional development—undergone by those who kept up with the leading edge of power led to economic and political change, at least some of which was wholly progressive. Institutional development was going on all the time including, for example, the expansion of bureaucracies and capacities for fiscal extraction, which paid for weapons with greater killing power. But what works at one time can lead to disaster in changed conditions. The dynamism of Europe certainly proved utterly destructive in modern conditions. What matters about those conditions is the entry of the people on to the political stage.

The people came in two forms, as workers and as nations. Neither of these had, to use the terms of Jean-Paul Sartre, essences; rather they had very different existences. This useful tag of social theory points to something very simple. Workers can and have been integrated into modern societies, members of the state rather than a class opposed to its very existence. The same point has been made about nations. Two processes are obvious about the integration of nations and states. The first has just been noted in connection with developments in England and France, namely a slow process whereby different nations acceded to a central unitary culture. Each state then had its own nation, with the nation having the protection of its own state. But, secondly, this harsh one to one reality is not the only one by means of which nations have been integrated in a state. Switzerland and India show that multinational nation-states can and do exist. Rights of all sorts—federal, consociational, and cultural—can give nations sufficient voice that they become loyal to a large political shell within which they can live.

But if integration is possible, so is the exclusion, as noted, that can lead to the politicization of class and nation, replete with the possibility of dire consequences. When states do not allow entry, through the granting of trade union or cultural rights, classes and nations, respectively, are likely to rise up and take on the state. Under these conditions, conflict intensifies rather than being diffused within the larger society. As we have also argued previously, allowing voice and accepting compromise is the best means to rule, for inclusion defangs radicalism. Europe's nineteenth-century regimes did not accept this, although Max Weber, the famous German sociologist, realized the importance of this principle in Germany. Anti-socialist laws had created a politically conscious class unnecessarily, given that liberalism had tamed the British working class.

---

[15]Nef (1963).

But one should not idealize the extent of either Weber's or Britain's understandings given the lack of imagination the thinker and the radical elements of the British state showed toward the national question. In both cases, there was great reluctance to contemplate any loss of state powers, either through making the state less unitary or by allowing downsizing. And there was a key linkage at work here: radical right elites feared socialism and so were tempted to play the national card against it.

Behind this fateful decision lay the firm belief that the size of the state was necessary for power. The fate of the Ottomans induced fear among the great European powers: as national groupings broke off, the weakness of the state became apparent. The great powers looked quite as much at both Russia and the United States and felt insecure for further reasons. Power in these states rested on secure sources of supply and on secure markets. It appeared that only this could allow geopolitical autonomy, so vitally necessary in a period of increasing geopolitical tension.

But herein lay the key dilemma of the late nineteenth century: if size was to be maintained in the circumstances of the time, as it had to be if power was to be preserved, it was also necessary to deal with the national question.[16] Accordingly, the great imperial centers sought to turn their composite monarchies into nation-states. Homogeneity would lend cohesion and power to the state, not least as it was believed that citizen armies had tremendous fighting spirit—as seemed to have been demonstrated by the Japanese when fighting Russia in 1905. Furthermore, homogeneity seemed necessary because a national minority might have an external national homeland, creating the possibility that it might, in war time, become a fifth column. Accordingly, state elites began to interfere with their peoples. There is ambiguity at this point. On occasion, it seems as if the actions of states actually created national movements where none existed before. But we have no desire to deny that some of these movements had already been formed, and that "official nationalisms" attempted to control something that they felt might get out of hand.[17] But in either case, the desire to homogenize gave nationalist movements a particular character, turning them from cultural affairs of professors into popular movements all-too-capable of political agency. The issues involved were evident in the pressures emerging within three imperial formations—Tsarist Russia, Austro-Hungary, and Great Britain.

Tsarist Russia felt threatened at the end of the nineteenth century even though others felt scared by its sheer size and especially by its reserves of manpower. If German military prowess and industrial power were scary, so was her alliance with Vienna, since this suggested an alliance between a single people. In these circumstances, radical state nationalists sought to enhance Russian power. Industrialization mattered but so too did the national question. Pure Russian ethnics were after all not a majority in the empire. But if Ukrainians could become Russian, that is, if they could be prevented from creating an identity of their own, then Russia might have the chance to create at least the core

---

[16]Lieven (1999).
[17]Anderson (1983), chap. 6.

of a nation-state. Harshness accordingly characterized Russian policy, and with it came certain unintended consequences. The Finns provide a classic instance of the way in which actions by a state can inadvertently change the character of pre-existing national feeling. Until the end of the century, the Finns had been content within the Tsarist Empire. They were largely left to their own devices, blessed with the liberties that came with the status of an imperial duchy. But the Tsar's rationalization policies, especially as they affected language, led a newly politicized nationalist movement to demand Finnish secession by the start of the twentieth century.

The world of Austro-Hungary at once resembled and differed from the Russian situation. Defeat by Germany had led to the granting of autonomy for the Magyars. They were not a majority in their own territory and so imposed very harsh assimilation conditions—close to success by 1914—on the Slovaks. The Austrian half of the empire, Cisleithenia, was very different. To begin with, German had simply seemed a world language to which other communities would accede. When this did not happen, when the Czechs started to gain political consciousness, the German community also gained consciousness as an ethnic group. But German ethnics were not a majority within Cisleithenia and certainly nothing like that in the empire as a whole. In these circumstances, the empire moved very slowly to a system of accommodation. This was a world of "bearable dissatisfaction" in the words of the Minister-President of Cisleithenia Count Taaffe, less a prison-house than a kindergarten of the nations. It is important to remember that no leader of the Czech national movement, to take but one example, sought actual independence during the nineteenth century—with key leaders such as Palacký arguing strongly against such a move, fearful of becoming a petty state exposed to German and Russian depradations. The Moravian Compromise looked set to secure loyalty through the granting of cultural rights, and something like this was being planned for the Czechs. But herein lay a major difficulty. The empire really needed a period of peace to consolidate such reforms, all of which were anyway undermining the powers of the central government. But the Hapsburgs wished to continue to play the great game of power politics. Their world was dominated by honor, making the thought of downsizing not just dangerous but morally humiliating. The Hapsburgs were accordingly suffering from what can only be termed political schizophrenia, forced to accommodate but attracted, in their heart of hearts, to homogenizing policies that would enhance their geopolitical strength.

At first sight, it might seem as if Great Britain represented the farthest opposite point to the Ottomans on a range measuring state strength. She ruled over large parts of the world, balanced her accounts and paid her military thanks to the contributions made by India, had at least some hegemonic powers, especially over the sea lanes, and was soon, during both world wars, able to call on reserves of manpower that did a good deal to bring victory. Nonetheless, the British elite felt under threat in structural terms. The country was after all but a small island, its possession of so much territory something of a freak. The defeat of the French in the great imperial contest of the late eighteenth and early nineteenth centuries had allowed Britain to expand, and the maintenance of its empire resulted thereafter from the exhaustion and then the balance between its

European rivals. But most of its rule was only skin deep. Weakness resulted in particular from what is now seen as one of its great achievements, free trade. Food had to be imported, making naval supremacy absolutely vital. It was this that made the German challenge—directed less at the acquisition of colonies than at the capacity to strike at the British fleet—so very scary, far more worrying than Germany's move toward the second industrial revolution.

One classic response was that of Sir John Seeley. It might well be the case that not everyone could be included in a larger British entity. This certainly applied to Africans but quite as much to Indians, even though key early Indian nationalists wanted to be part of a larger Britannic entity. The empire had racial discrimination at its core, at least in its later stages, so Seeley's dream was for a Greater Britain based on the white settlers of Australia, Canada, South Africa, and New Zealand. There was a measure of shared identity in the white Dominions. But these plans nonetheless came to naught for at least two reasons. First, the settlers were proud and independent, not at all keen to respond to calls for imperial defense given their own needs and ever more irritated by foreign policy being decided in London. In this general context, it is important to remember Ireland. The varied plans for Home Rule stalemated British politics at the end of the nineteenth century and beyond, all without success. Indeed, in 1914, Britain faced the possibility of mutiny in its own army, reluctant to allow a minority of Protestants to be included in Home Rule for the whole, largely Catholic island of Ireland and viscerally opposed to anything that would undermine the unity of the empire.[18] Second, the idea of imperial unity often had at its core tariff reform, that is, the creation of a closed imperial trading bloc. There was powerful resistance to this, for it seemed to guarantee more expensive food.[19] Empire might be popular in a vague way but not when it came to affect the living standards of the people. In the end, then, schemes for a federal empire came to naught because there was insufficient interest on either side.

Resolution of these issues came to a head through the world wars. By the end of the nineteenth century European territory was, so to speak, filled up, allowing no further expansion on the continent. In these circumstances, war would necessarily be a disaster. But the intensity of geopolitical competition and the enormous insecurities of the great powers meant that the desire for complete autonomy was rampant. The great powers accordingly felt themselves to be dependent on the possession of huge swathes of territory. The picture as a whole is best characterized as the marriage of nationalism and imperialism. Each state sought secure sources of supply and secure outlets for goods produced. At any particular moment in time, this might seem silly, given that the British Empire allowed others to trade with its territories before 1914. But that might change, as was obvious to those on the continent looking at British politicians from both parties who were talking about the need for imperial union. Let us turn to the way in which the bundle of issues–empire, state size, nationalism, and power—played out in practice.

---

[18]Lieven (1999).
[19]Trentmann (2008).

We will make two points, the first a negative, the second drawing a distinction between the character of the two world wars.

The negative point is very simple. It is not the case that the struggle for possessions overseas led in any immediate way to World War I. For, what always mattered most to the great powers was their security within the European heartland—and, more particularly, their determination not to let matters get so out of hand again that anything like the strains and stresses of the revolutionary and Napoleonic period would be repeated.[20] It was this background condition that made it relatively easy to settle imperial disputes, especially over the partition of Africa, which took place in the 1880s. After all, imperial possessions paid little—with the exception of India, which, as noted, mattered enormously for Britain. The balance within Europe is the factor that allowed Britain to gain a huge empire in the first place. Similarly, geopolitical factors do most to explain its longevity—French resentments were never likely to lead to war given the increasing power of Germany, while Germany itself for long did not wish to increase French and Russian power at the expense of Britain since that would weaken its own position. Besides, the British Empire was, as noted, open to trade from its rivals. In summary, imperial disputes before 1914 were always kept within bounds; they certainly did not actually cause the onset of disaster. Nonetheless, Germany clearly felt left out, receiving the merest trifles despite an activist foreign policy under Kaiser Wilhelm II.

Our second point is about the difference between the two world wars. While full agreement as to the origins of the First World War will never be achieved, some comments can be made that relate to the argument made to this point. Nationalism most certainly played some part in the origin of the war. Most immediately, the occasion for war was the shots fired by the Serbian nationalist Gavrilo Princip, an irredentist nationalist keen to establish a Greater Serbia. More generally there were traces of the marriage of nationalism and imperialism, not just in an intellectual like Weber but also in the mind of the German Chancellor Bethmann-Hollweg. Still more important were the feelings in Vienna. The stiff note sent to Serbia that demanded oversight of its internal affairs, backed by Germany, was in part caused by the fear that the empire would not be able to compete in a world in which size and national homogeneity mattered so much if it could not control its own territory—that is, if secession by the southern Slavs meant that its power would be undermined, as had been true of that of the Ottomans.

Nevertheless, World War I also had the character of a normal interstate conflict within a multipolar system. Two basic factors tend to explain escalation to the extremes in a system of states.[21] The first is that of heterogeneity in the system as a whole, the presence of different values making mutual understanding difficult. This was certainly present by 1914 in a way that it had not been when Bismarck and Lord Salisbury were conducting the foreign policies of their respective countries. The second is that of the character of the states involved, that is, establishing whether they had the institutional capacity—so often

---

[20]Darwin (2007).
[21]Hall (1996).

presumed by realism to exist—to calculate rationally. There were clear deficiencies at the time. While the British state had brilliantly retrenched so as to face Germany, domestic politics made it impossible to give Germany the warning—by means of an open alliance with France—that might have prevented conflict. The Hapsburg case was made endlessly difficult by Hungarian autonomy. But the key variable involved was the inability of the German state to calculate rationally. For one thing, middle-class nationalists such as Weber were pressing their state for a more activist policy. But the crucial factor was that the state was really a court, with policy determined by whoever had last gained the ear of the Kaiser and with no priority set between a world policy directed against England and the traditional Eastern policy directed against Russia.[22] The famous "Memorandum on the Present State of British Relations with France and Germany" penned by Eyre Crowe on January 1, 1907, argued that this explained German behavior as well as any purportedly conscious, aggressive planning:

> It might be suggested that the great German design is in reality no more than the expression of a vague, confused, and unpractical statesmanship, not fully realizing its own drift. A charitable critic might add, by way of explanation, that the well-known qualities of mind and temperament distinguishing for good or for evil the present Ruler of Germany may not improbably be largely responsible for the erratic, domineering, and often frankly aggressive spirit which is recognizable at present in every branch of German public life ... and that this spirit has called forth those manifestations of discontent and alarm both at home and abroad with which the world is becoming familiar; that, in fact, Germany does not really know what she is driving at, and that all her excursions and alarms, all her underhand intrigues do not contribute to the steady working out of a well-conceived and relentlessly followed system of policy, because they do not really form part of any such system.[23]

Werner Sombart suggested that the real choice facing Germany was between geopolitical heroism and trade, with the latter in fact being far more rational given that Germany had become the largest economy in Europe in 1913—without the benefit of imperial possessions. As it turned out, however, the heroic frame of mind won out and led to a final dreadful miscalculation, that of letting loose submarines on American shipping. Without that, Germany might have been able to establish hegemony on the continent given the collapse of Russia in 1917.

Industry applied to war together with grand justifications to legitimize conscription ("a war to end all wars," "a war for democracy," the promise of "a land fit for heroes") meant that conflict escalated so as to make it savagely destructive and, with the benefit of hindsight, no longer a rational policy for the states concerned. As institutions

---

[22]Mann (1993), chap. 21.
[23]Crowe (1928), p. 415.

were destroyed, everything changed. Defeat in war so weakened the Tsarist Empire that workers and peasants destroyed the polity. If this is to stress the impact of class, ethnicity mattered as well. The empire was of course recreated under new management, a significant part of it Jewish in background, as figures of this sort found that national liberation meant their eventual exclusion, thereby turning them into left-wing empire savers.[24] The Nazi revolution came later, but it too resulted from the breakdown of institutions and the emergence of radical right nationalists, furious at the humiliations they felt had been imposed on Germany.

This suggests the crucial point that the caging of nations becomes impossible only when states are thrown into disarray, characteristically by defeat in war. Further, the nationalist movements that then took over had gained political consciousness because of the way in which states had treated them—with Masaryk becoming certain of the need for full independence only very late and partly in response to the new emperor's plan to "Germanify" Cisleithenia. Put differently, were it not for the intensity of geopolitical competition, it is possible that the nationalities problem in some places, above all in Cisleithenia, might have been solved in such a way as to allow for several nations to live under a single but necessarily more liberal political roof. As it was, the new nation-states that emerged in Central Europe were feeble, often in conflict with each other and filled with nationalities problems of their own.

Central Europe then became a power vacuum into which larger states were always likely to be drawn. All this made it impossible to create a sustainable geopolitical settlement in the interwar period. These conditions also contributed to the onset of the Great Depression and the consequent increasing salience of the politics of economic autarchy. But if protectionism increased international disorder, as Cordell Hull believed, it is as well to remember that protectionism was itself caused by a failure to create order in the world polity. It was in these circumstances that the marriage of nationalism and imperialism became ever more important. Japan exemplifies this trend, feeling that the Southeast Asia co-prosperity zone was necessary for survival given the lack of its own sources of oil. One element that went into the mix in Germany was the experience by 1918 of food shortages, caused by the British blockade. This certainly made the possession of territory attractive. Both Japan and Germany were aggressive, imperial states, and this made World War II utterly different in character from World War I. World War II was an inter-imperial war of territorial expansion rather than the traditional conflict that began in 1914 in which, at the start, every state claimed war was necessary for defense. But one cannot leave the matter at this point. For the uniqueness of the German situation was the desire for *Lebensraum*, for an expansion within Europe that would not create, as had traditionally been the case, a multinational polity. The intent was rather to kill and cleanse so that only Aryans would inhabit the conquered territories. The ultimate perversion of nationalism was the polity envisaged by Hitler in which extermination of difference would allow extension of a single race.

---

[24]Riga (2012).

Recovery

The fundamental source of stability in the early postwar years was the freezing of the international nation-state system consequent on the emergence of two great nuclear powers, both fully aware that war to the extremes had become genuinely irrational, as it would lead to total destruction. Toward the end of the war, Stalin had suggested that the postwar world would witness the normal historical process: each side would establish its own system on the territory it controlled. There is much to recommend this pithy judgment. Fears on both sides of the potential universalizing military drives of its rival led to the peace being essentially warlike, marked by a continual arms race and by a large number of proxy wars. But the two states were soon "enemy partners." Even at the start it was noticeable that both disapproved of European colonialism. Over time, each side recognized that the other was not seeking to overturn the ordering of the world polity. Tensions could be extreme as the Berlin wall and the Cuban missile crisis illustrated. But what was most noticeable was essential restraint in the bipolar relationship. And order most certainly was present within their respective social worlds.

In the Soviet case, there was never much doubt but that order rested on coercion. The armies of the Warsaw Pact were present throughout Eastern and Central Europe, and they were used in Hungary in 1956 and in Czechoslovakia in 1968 to ensure continued control from Moscow. All of these communist states were repulsive, all prison houses, though some were far less oppressive than others. Insofar as the Soviet Bloc represented a system, it was, however, in the end bound to be unstable. For one thing, no new Soviet sense of belonging ever really emerged, making the repression of nationalist demands ever more difficult to maintain—in the long run costing the center far more than it was able to extract from its periphery. For another thing, the empire contained within it social formations at very different levels of social and political evolution. Bluntly, instability was inevitable for Moscow because the empire contained the fiercely nationalist Poles and Baltic states which had experienced independence in the interwar years. But such sources of instability were successfully contained for a long time.

The situation in the affluent capitalist world was wholly different. In Europe, three factors were particularly important. First, the majority of states changed their character, as can best be seen by looking at the way in which Europe became a zone of peace. Let us remember that politicization is caused by exclusion, by being forced to take on the state. This was by and large no longer true in Western Europe after 1945 in regard to nationalism. Ethnic cleansing, population transfer, and genocide had so homogenized states as to remove most nationalities problems. Liberalism flourished, in other words, on the back of horror—a process revisited in recent years in the third set of Balkan wars. An essential basis for belonging had been created. The same political principle affected class. The extreme right had been destroyed by war, while the left was undermined in the immediate postwar period, in part through American actions. Hence, an historic class compromise was possible, thanks above all to the workings of Christian Democracy, allowing class relations to take place within the system rather than in opposition to it.[25] Further, the Europeans made a major contribution to economic recovery both through their own investments and by creating welfare institutions, such as social security and unemployment insurance systems, that provided the social cement allowing greater utilization of the market principle—and which enhanced the sense of belonging to society.[26]

Second, and perhaps more important, was the realization that the attempt to be complete power containers had led to complete disaster. This produced humility, a becoming sense of modesty. But this is *not* to say that state power somehow lost its salience. The crucial calculation was that of France—and it was clearly realist.[27] If Germany could not be beaten militarily, an alternative strategy might be possible: a permanent embrace of mutual cooperation could neutralize aggression. The origin of what is now the EU came from the 1950 decision by the two leading powers to give up their geopolitical autonomy by establishing genuine interdependence in coal and steel, thereby giving up the capacity to make their own weapons. Trade took the place of heroism. The condominium between these two powers has structured the EU throughout its history. Soon, the negative realist calculation blended into something positive, endorsed by many more countries. States discovered that giving up the desire to control everything in fact gave them more: interdependence within a larger security frame allowed for prosperity and the spread of citizenship rights. Put differently, breaking the link between nationalism and imperialism enhanced rather than undermined state power. And this too led to institution building.

If these calculations were fundamental, they did not dictate the political form that resulted. The group around Jean Monnet had drafted the agreement around coal and steel, and it was as involved in drawing up the plans for the European Economic Community, formed in 1957. Their dream was federalist, seen above all in the creation of a Commission, a Parliament, and a Court. Monnet was highly cosmopolitan, a high-flying representative of international finance. Accordingly, the plans he developed privileged economic liberalism—something that then came to dominate European integration thereafter. But how was it that a group of French bureaucrats, albeit in league with colleagues in other countries, came to have sufficient power to change Europe's constitutional structure? One element was certainly geopolitical, namely the discovery by France at the time of Suez that British power was exhausted and that a measure of autonomy could only be guaranteed through cooperation with Germany.

But a third factor was at work that allowed for the creation of a new Europe after 1945. Europe's security dilemma at last found a solution in the years following the close of World War II. One element of this was the creation of an "empire by invitation."[28] The

---

[25]Kaiser (2007).

[26]Milward (1984). In some cases, the postwar era solidified class compromises begun earlier during the Great Depression. These cases included in particular the Scandinavian countries but also the United States where certain instances of corporatism were attempted under the National Recovery Act until the Supreme Court struck them down.

[27]Milward (1992).

[28]Lundestad (1986).

formulation of Lord Ismay—that the purpose of NATO was to keep the Russians out, the Americans in, and the Germans divided—bears repetition. The Russian threat was real, felt as acutely by those on the front line as it was in Washington. It was this that led the Americans to take active steps to remove the extreme left of European politics in the years immediately after 1945—taking particular care, for instance, to support Christian Democracy in Italy against its communist rivals.[29] Of course, Europeans appreciated the American presence for an entirely different reason. They had fought endlessly and to the point of absolute exhaustion. The United States was to act as an umpire or court of last appeal. When distrust is very high there is a great deal to be said for a mediator—and one in this case possessed of powerful means of coercion and persuasion. The decision to keep Germany divided exemplifies the difference between the way the First and Second World Wars ended: power mattered in 1945, not least since obeisance before the principle of national self-determination in 1919 was considered to have contributed to geopolitical disaster. Geopolitical stability is a precondition for investment and economic growth. Just as interdependence was undermined by geopolitical competition in the interwar period, so too was it made possible within Europe after 1945, because a stable international order had been put in place. The ability of states to become traders rather than heroes rested on secure geopolitical foundations. And it is at this point that we can complete the explanation for the impact of federalism within Europe. At key points in his career, Monnet drew on his influence within the United States to push European integration forward.[30] The desire to create a new Europe was as present in Washington as in its allies, albeit in the American case overwhelmingly for geopolitical reasons, and the construction would not have taken place without its pressure—and its forbearance, seen above all in the acceptance of a European model of "embedded liberalism" that it did not itself favor.

That the United States had such an impact is easy to explain. The baseline was the enormous economic power of the United States in the immediate postwar years. Mobilization for war facilitated the growth of manufacturing in virtually all of its major industries as well as much institutional state building. So did the fact that much of Europe and Japan lay in ruins after the war and needed products that were not readily available at home thanks to the devastation of their own manufacturing capacities. American firms were more than happy to fill the gap. By the early 1960s, American companies accounted for well over 90 percent of all sales in autos, steel, industrial chemicals, consumer electronics, apparel, footwear, electrical components, and machine tools within the domestic market. They also held substantial market shares abroad. They provided over 20 percent of all the world's exports in key industries, such as aircraft, motor vehicles, telecommunications equipment, plastics, machine tools, agricultural machinery, medical and pharmaceutical products, railway vehicles, and housing fixtures.[31] By the mid-1970s, 211 of the 401 largest manufacturing enterprises in the

---

[29]Maier (1981).
[30]Anderson (2009).
[31]Zucker et al. (1982), p. 14.

world were American.[32] Not surprisingly, then, America was an export giant of goods and services as well as capital to the rest of the world.[33] Nevertheless, economic growth was driven mostly by domestic demand. By 1970, the value of exports was only 4.4 percent of its GDP.[34]

Behind this success lay America's Fordist production model. Named after Henry Ford who pioneered mass production techniques in the automobile industry, Fordism involved large, vertically integrated corporations. The Ford Motor Company, for instance, eventually owned forests, iron and coal mines, limestone quarries, Brazilian rubber plantations, and a fleet of freighters as well as a regional railroad to bring it all to Ford production facilities where the company manufactured virtually all of the materials and components necessary to build its cars and trucks. Firms like these specialized in producing for mass markets and so could take advantage of economies of scale. Workers for these firms were often organized in labor unions that had struck agreements with their employers to tie wage increases to productivity increases. This capital-labor accord, forged in the late 1940s, remained in place for another thirty years. The final piece of the Fordist model involved state spending. Although relatively limited by West European standards, the American welfare state helped bolster the mass consumption required to sustain mass production. So did the military, which purchased all manner of goods, from attaché cases to zippers, from private manufacturers.[35] The government also made major investments in infrastructure, notably President Eisenhower's commitment to a national interstate highway system. Total state spending rose steadily from 11.6 percent of GDP ($281 billion) in 1948 to 21.3 percent of GDP ($1.15 trillion) by 1975. 30.6 percent of federal state expenditures went toward national defense in 1948, rising to a peak of 69.5 percent in 1954 and then falling back to 26.0 percent in 1975.[36] Prosperity resulted. Unemployment in the 1960s and early 1970s ran from between 4 percent to 6 percent of the labor force. Average wages grew about 2.5 percent per year as did increases in labor productivity. Poverty rates dropped from roughly 22 percent to 11 percent of the population during the same time. Wage inequality remained fairly stable and considerably lower than it is today.[37]

A well-known and genuinely important theory suggests that capitalist society works well when a single liberal hegemonic power fulfills certain functions for the system as a whole—most notably, insisting on free trade, providing a top currency and defense, and sending capital out so that the world can develop.[38] The theory sometimes suggests that Great Britain was once a hegemonic leader of this sort, noting too that the burden

---

[32]Chandler (1992), p. 136.

[33]America's current account balance during the 1960s and early 1970s was in surplus (U.S. Federal Reserve 2013a).

[34]U.S. Department of Commerce (1975), part 2, p. 886.

[35]Piore and Sabel (1984).

[36]U.S. Office of Management and Budget (2013), Historical Tables 3.1, 3.1. Dollar figures are in constant 2005FY dollars.

[37]Mishel et al. (2012), pp. 77, 179, 335, 422.

[38]Gilpin (1981). The theory in question is perhaps too economistic. The United States has also sought to prevent nuclear proliferation, a purely geopolitical concern.

on defense for others had much to do with its decline. There is almost no truth to that specific claim. Britain was but one power among others, and it certainly did not have the military capacity to push through an agenda of free trade. In contrast, the United States has had genuine hegemonic powers within capitalism—and eventually world-wide once the Soviet Union collapsed. The fact that it produced nearly 50 percent of total world product in 1945 allowed it to create much of the architecture of the world economy in its own image.

At Bretton Woods, Harry Dexter White used sheer political muscle to ensure the dominance of the United States.[39] First, he guaranteed that the United States controlled the key positions in the world's most important transnational economic organizations—the International Monetary Fund (IMF) and the World Bank. The former was to provide loans to countries suffering from debt and balance of payments problems, the latter to finance infrastructure development projects for countries in need. Because the United States was the primary financial contributor to these organizations—a direct result of its economic might when they were first set up—it enjoyed considerable leverage as to which countries were to receive assistance and the conditions under which it was to be given.[40] Second, decisions made at Bretton Woods established an international free-trade regime under the rubric of the General Agreement on Tariffs and Trade (GATT), which later became the World Trade Organization (WTO). This was something the British delegation at Bretton Woods, led by John Maynard Keynes, desperately wanted to avoid because it would destroy the preferential trade relations Britain had enjoyed within its empire. But a free-trade regime suited the United States: its firms and investors could profit handsomely from easier access to the empire's markets. This drove an economic stake into the heart of Britain, already reeling economically from the costs of war, which now lost whatever remaining hope it had of preserving its empire.[41] Finally, foreign currencies would be convertible into gold at the equivalent of $35 per ounce—the so-called Gold Window. But since gold was in short supply, US dollars could be substituted. This meant that the dollar became the world's reserve currency, thereby giving the United States seigniorage privileges.

Some such privileges were so to speak innocent, most notably the ability to borrow at lower interest rates in large part because the world's commodities were priced in dollars. But some were, as the French had it, "exorbitant." Control over the dollar gave America the power to print money more or less as it saw fit, with other countries feeling obliged to hang on to dollars either through geopolitical or economic calculation. So seigniorage allowed America to easily increase the money supply or borrow and incur debt.[42] When

---

[39]Steil (2013).

[40]Pauly (1997). Emblematic of US influence is the fact that the president appoints the head of the World Bank.

[41]Pauly (1997); Skidelsky (2000).

[42]"Printing money" is a term often used by the media, central bankers, financial analysts, and others to describe a variety of monetary policy maneuvers. Typically it involves creating new money to finance government deficits or pay off government debt. Lyndon Johnson's administration did this to pay for the Vietnam War. But it can also serve to pump liquidity into the economy when necessary. Barack Obama's administration did so by printing money with which it bought back government bonds, a process known as quantitative easing.

some of those countries generated huge surpluses of their own, the potential for danger as the result of global financial imbalances arose. For money likes to go somewhere; excessive lending has the potential to fuel dangerous bubbles. Those developments lay in the future, but the point to be made about the postwar settlement is that it was incomplete. Keynes had a much more complete plan, one designed to discipline creditor as well as debtor countries, but this was rejected by the United States, not surprisingly given its massive creditor status at the end of the war. And we can add a detail. If capitalism as a whole is likely to suffer from problems caused by global imbalances, so too is the EU—a smaller currency area, of course, but one in which Germany's massive surplus has to find outlets. The relations between power and money, always close, will concern us a great deal in the rest of this book.

It is entirely clear that the United States chose to knock Great Britain off its perch at the end of the war, aware that it had the capacity to be the leading power and keen to rise to the occasion. Still, what is noticeable about the early years of American hegemony within capitalism was that the exercise of power was relatively benign within the core capitalist countries, although not always within the developing world. The American economy was a powerhouse during the postwar period and fueled much of the international economy. Further, the government helped by providing $13 billion in aid through its Marshall Plan to rebuild war-devastated regions in Europe—albeit aid that was conditional upon recipient countries agreeing to decontrol prices, stabilize exchange rates, and balance budgets. Whether US power would be used differently once its economic dominance was challenged is a question we explore in later chapters.

CHAPTER 2
CONDITIONS OF EXISTENCE, OLD AND NEW

Human history does not come neatly packaged in precise and sharply delineated boundaries. This is certainly true of the world in which states now exist both as objects and subjects. We turn first to a series of novelties, occurring at different times and with different levels of intensity, that have done a very great deal to create new conditions of existence within which states now have to live. But the past is to some extent the present and the future too, as the American playwright Eugene O'Neill stressed; so attention then turns to continuities of structure and behavior, to patterns of social life familiar to us from what we have said in the previous chapter about the past. A consideration of both leads to a conclusion that characterizes the nature of our world today. By explaining the general conditions—both old and new—within which states operate today, our discussion in this chapter provides a bridge from the last chapter, which gave a sweeping account of the development of states in light of their need to provide order, security and belonging, to the next four, which discuss different species of states today.

Novelties

One fundamental change that distinguishes the past from the present stands out from all others because it is both qualitative and irreversible. The horrors of Hiroshima and Nagasaki made it clear that a fundamental jump had taken place in the killing capacity of weapons. The result was seen in Khrushchev's comment that the atomic bomb does not distinguish between social classes—a declaration admitting that war was now absolutely irrational between the greatest two powers. Further acknowledgment of this fact came in the early 1960s when the United States encouraged the Soviets to have second-strike capacity in their nuclear arsenal. The possession solely of first-strike capacity was dangerous in that it might encourage them to launch first—an eventuality that might then push the United States into an early strike of its own. Confidence that mutually assured destruction (MAD) has worked can never be total. Policymakers have threatened the use of these weapons, not least on two occasions when Henry Kissinger, who ought to have known better, played a dominant role in the conduct of American foreign policy. Further, states without second-strike capacity do sometimes threaten to use them, as has been true recently of North Korea. This would be sheer lunacy as it might well lead to the total destruction of their own societies—but human folly has been all-too-present in the historical record, although never on such scale. Finally, we are far from free from fears of accidents. Writers and filmmakers have depicted nuclear catastrophe for decades, notably in Sidney Lumet's cold war movie thriller, *Failsafe*, which showed an accidental thermonuclear first-strike by the United States on Moscow. The complex nature of the technological systems involved could turn fiction into reality, as nearly happened on at least one occasion.[1]

That war is unlikely between the greatest powers is utterly remarkable, and wonderful news for humanity, given the disasters caused by the world wars. A good deal of further optimism can be found in a second change within the postwar world political economy. Communicative capacities are establishing ever-closer linkages across the globe. It is very important, given that pundits have recently so often imagined that globalization will curtail the power of states, to begin by stressing something rather different. A fundamental element to globalization is that of the spread of the ideal of the nation-state. Empires have fallen, first of course in South America and then after World War I, but still more so with decolonization and the collapse of the Soviet bloc. There are, so to speak, good and bad points to be made about this. The good news is that of the spread of the norm of non-intervention—the belief that territorial integrity must be maintained. The norm has been broken most often by great powers in the postwar world both through proxy wars and direct interventions of their own. In contrast, new states, especially those that contain many ethnicities, some with kin outside their borders, have overwhelmingly endorsed the norm. When borders are wholly irrational, they must be maintained. We emphasize later in this book that state and nation building cannot now take place, as they did in European history, through inter-state conflict—a development about which one can have ambivalent feelings. The certain bad news is that the large number of conflicts within states—forming the great proportion of wars in the last quarter century—have on occasion been bloody and vicious, particularly when these have taken place within Central Africa. This is the world of predatory states, often supported with funds from the outside, in which the hold of an elite on power is so tenuous that immediate extraction of benefits seems necessary. Child soldiers, excessively weak states, and easily exploitable resources have produced modern horror in places like Rwanda and Uganda. So, we have in all this a basic contrast between a world of relative peace in the North and of considerable conflict in various parts of the South.

Still, when one reflects on the era of imperialism, it becomes obvious that the situation in the South would be far more conflictual were it still the case that the advanced powers felt it necessary to gain territorial possessions overseas. But the belief that size is necessary to secure prosperity—to control sources of supply and obtain large markets, and to possess a large population for military purposes—has diminished in the most striking manner at least among the advanced states. It was always going to be almost impossible for the great imperial powers to maintain their empires in the face of the rise of nationalism, but the fear that the loss of territory would lead to poverty meant that vicious resistance to downsizing was mounted on occasion. Key elements of the French army felt that their future would lead to decline as surely as had the loss of territory led

---

[1]Schlosser (2013).

to decline in Spain. So, they mounted a hideous war in Algeria—together with attempted assassination of their own President. A vital intellectual argument made in the midst of this war, Raymond Aron's *La tragédie algérienne*, pointed out that the dream of imperial reformers—to make a larger France of genuinely shared citizenship—could not be realized without huge cost: raising the standard of living of the Arab majority in North Africa would have sharply diminished that of Parisians.[2]

An important discovery followed from decolonization. The advanced world's prosperity improved rapidly, essentially by trading with itself. The glorious years of economic growth that followed decolonization showed that empire was not necessary. One can go a little further in saying that the world economy has so changed its character that there are very good reasons to believe that conquest will now bring few benefits.[3] If the costs of resistance are clear, so too is the sheer difficulty of capturing the leading edge of technology through the possession of territory. Human capital matters and it is highly mobile; so too are many factors of production at the higher more profitable end of the scale. There is also another side to the equation. One can access important economic knowledge and production through non-territorial activity. Foreign direct investment (FDI) is one such source; another is that of alliances between firms.

This general point is of such importance that it must be highlighted. The secret to success in late industrial society seems to be that of intensification, the creation of human capital able to respond to technological change. According to the World Economic Forum (WEF), seven of the top fifteen most competitive economies in the world in 2013 were small countries such as Switzerland, Singapore, Finland, Taiwan, and Denmark. Their success stemmed not only from a well-educated labor force but also from the fact that they had well-developed states with strong public institutions, sound property rights, low levels of corruption, and efficient government.[4] Brains now matter more than brawn.

With these factors in mind, let us consider the nature of contemporary capitalism, the larger sea within which states now have to swim. Two portraits are in order: one about economic developments, another about the exercise of power—the first appearing the more important to one of us, the second mattering most to the other!

An initial portrayal can usefully be aseptic, even static. First, there was an explosion in trade and capital mobility across national borders beginning in the 1970s and accelerating in the 1990s. For instance, in the mid-1980s, growth of international trade began accelerating faster than the growth of world GDP.[5] Secondly, as barriers to capital mobility disappeared, the world experienced dramatic increases in FDI. This was driven in part by petrodollars from oil producing countries flooding into the world economy after 1973, thanks to sharp increases in oil prices worldwide. In countries around the world policy restrictions on cross-border capital flows declined substantially in the

---

[2] Aron (1957).
[3] Brooks (2005).
[4] World Economic Forum (2013).
[5] Centeno and Cohen (2010), p. 46.

1980s and 1990s. The most striking development was the rapid march among North American and West European countries toward virtually total financial openness. With the exception of the Middle East and South Asia, other regions followed this trend.[6] From the 1980s through the 2000s, gross FDI rose steadily from about 1 percent to 4 percent of GDP worldwide.[7] Even more impressive were the increases in portfolio investment, including trade in stocks, bonds, and foreign currencies, which by 1993 were three times as large as FDI within the OECD countries.[8] Finally, corporations increasingly outsourced production and other tasks to companies around the world. Firms developed more decentralized and networked organizational forms that transcended national boarders, such as inter-firm alliances, joint ventures, and global commodity chains.[9] To an increasing extent, since the early 1990s, the multinational firms engaged in this sort of activity were emerging from countries outside the advanced capitalist core.[10] Much of this was made possible by dramatic improvements in information and telecommunications technologies that facilitated nearly instantaneous transactions worldwide as well as vast improvements in transportation such as the advent of just-in-time overnight delivery service to most anywhere in the world.

This portrait needs to be complemented by another, stressing the realities of power. We offer two considerations. First, one must note a change in the character of American hegemony in the capitalist world. We have seen that hegemonic power was initially exercised benignly within the advanced capitalist world, most notably in the monies provided for the Marshall Plan. But the funds needed for the Great Society program and for war in Vietnam led not to higher taxation but to the printing of huge numbers of dollars, thereby doing a good deal to cause the great postwar inflation of the 1970s. The architecture of the world economy accordingly changed in an instant—from a fixed and stable system to one in which currencies floated, at times against each other. This change is a basic novelty within the postwar world. It has however become apparent that the United States retains its privileges because capitalist society still depends on the dollar. Europe may have resisted holding dollars, but allied countries such as Saudi Arabia and Japan have chosen to do so to support the country that protects them—with China's vast dollar reserves resting on more opportunistic calculations. This is the dangerous world of global imbalances. In general, seigniorage has become severe, the ability to extract resources from the world. Consider the management of the dollar. The United States has at times diminished the value of the dollar by recourse to its printing press, and this has allowed for economic recovery as American exports become cheaper, notably in the mid-1980s and again after 2008. But recovery brings in its turn a stronger dollar. This has been disastrous for others. The "original sin" of many developing countries lies in the need to borrow capital in a currency that is not their own, which they did massively

---

[6]Simmons et al. (2008).
[7]Centeno and Cohen (2010), p. 80.
[8]Campbell (2003).
[9]Gereffi (1994); Gulati and Gargiulo (1999); Powell (1987).
[10]Guillén and García-Canal (2010); Hopewell (2013).

from the 1970s.[11] Real difficulties ensue when the dollar strengthens, leading much of the world to complain of currency manipulation.

This weakness within the developing world points to the second consideration about power. The North dominates the world political economy. Much of the increase in trade occurred in the so-called triad region of North America, Western Europe, and Japan. In the mid-1990s, nearly 90 percent of the merchandise imports and exports of the world were traded within the triad. Most of this trade happened among countries within rather than between triad regions—particularly among countries within Western Europe. Much the same is true today. Indeed, nowadays the United States, China, Japan, Germany, and Canada account for nearly half of all world trade.[12] The same is true of FDI. Through 2011, the advanced capitalist countries absorbed over half of the world's inflows of FDI and generated nearly 60 percent of the world's outflows of FDI.[13] A single image of Northern power concerns the iPhone and iPad: these marvels of technology and huge source of profit have less than 5 percent of their value added in China where they are assembled.[14] As with many high tech products, profits derive from software rather than hardware—which is to say that profits go to the designers in the North, not to the cheap labor of the South.

All orders have costs and benefits attached, and contemporary capitalism is far from "just." Still, in historical perspective, an initial point is very noticeable: the capitalist world now has a rich institutional character, not just in the key arenas of the International Monetary Fund, the World Bank and the World Trade Organization, but in thousands of international organizations, often centered on the United Nations (UN). Such depth diminishes the possibility of conflict. The demands of rising powers can be accommodated and met by institutional embraces. But this does not mean that we should ignore signs of some diminution in Northern dominance. First, in 2011 the low-wage, energy-exporting countries of China, Russia, Saudi Arabia, Singapore, Kuwait, South Korea, Malaysia, Thailand, Indonesia, Qatar, Nigeria, Venezuela, and Libya had a collective current account surplus of about $753 billion, or 10.6 percent of their GDP. By comparison that same year, the United States, Canada, and the EU had a collective current account deficit of about $629 billion.[15] Second, in 2012, for the first time ever, the developing world absorbed more FDI (51 percent of the world total) than the advanced capitalist countries, suggesting that investment opportunities were shifting regionally. The developing world's contribution to FDI is also rising and hit a record high of 31 percent in 2012, which suggests that investment capital can be raised to a greater extent outside the triad region than ever before.[16] Third, this reflects the fact, already noted, that more and more multinational firms are from the newly industrializing countries. Nearly 30 percent of the

---

[11] In less than two decades, the world's most indebted countries jumped from owing 10 percent to nearly 48 percent of their GDP to foreign creditors (Centeno and Cohen 2010), pp. 75–79.
[12] Centeno and Cohen (2010), chap. 2; Fligstein (2001), pp. 199–200.
[13] UNCTAD (2013).
[14] Worstall (2011).
[15] Alpert (2013), chap. 2.
[16] UNCTAD (2013).

world's multinationals are now headquartered in developing countries. Many are making tremendous inroads into markets traditionally dominated by multinationals from the North: the world's largest candy maker is Arcor of Argentina, the largest bakery is Bimbo of Mexico, the largest manufacturer of regional jets is Embraer of Brazil, and the largest energy company (excluding oil companies) is Gazprom of Russia. Further, many of the emerging multinationals have turned acquisitive: Tata Steel of India purchased Britain's Corus Group, Geradau of Brazil purchased Chaparral Steel in the United States, SABIC of Saudi Arabia acquired GE Plastics in the United States, and Industrial and Commercial Bank of China purchased Standard Bank Group in South Africa.[17] All of this is to say that the world is now a smaller place—in which oversupply and excess capacity of labor, plants, equipment, and goods and services may yet cause fundamental problems.[18]

Two final features of today's world set it apart from the first half of the twentieth century: the collapse of the Soviet Union and the rise of neoliberalism. The two are related insofar as the collapse of an alternative model to capitalism gave particular salience to neoliberalism.

The causes of the collapse of the Soviet Union are not as yet completely clear. But any complete account is likely to include the following elements. The first is that the attempt to liberalize the socialist system failed for a simple reason. Decompression of a regime requires partners and skill. The former were lacking in socialist society given that secondary associations such as unions and business organizations simply did not exist. Gorbachov wanted to make bargains, but he had no interlocutors. This in itself made it likely that demands would escalate—all the more so, of course, given the belief that *glasnost* (i.e., permitting open discussion of political issues) was a necessary step to *perestroika* (i.e., economic and government reform). Alexis de Tocqueville's brilliant analysis of the French revolution made clear that a revolutionary situation is created by rising demands that are then suddenly blocked. The moral is clear: it is necessary to keep one's nerve when challenges come in, rather than to seek to put the genie of discontent back into the bottle. But Gorbachov opened the system and then sought to close it down again, thereby acting unbeknownst to himself as the perfect gravedigger of the system he had sought to save. The way in which he did so deserves note, namely that of allowing nationalist mobilizations before then seeking to control them by sudden acts of repression in Georgia and the Baltics. This points to the simplest of all considerations. The collapse of the Soviet Union was the last act of decolonization, the ending of a traditional Russian empire recreated under different leadership after World War I and then massively expanded at the end of World War II, thanks to the prowess of the Red Army. The collapse created the unipolar "moment" of American power with which the world has had to live for the last quarter century. One element of that power has been the neoliberal views endorsed and spread by the United States.

During much of the second half of the twentieth century, Keynesianism dominated policymaking circles in the capitalist world. Lessons learned from Roosevelt's New Deal

---

[17]Guillén and Ontiveros (2012), chap. 3.
[18]Alpert (2013).

created a postwar environment that was more than amenable to Keynesianism. In brief, the idea was that the state could deploy fiscal and monetary policies in ways that would modulate aggregate demand, smooth out business cycles, and avoid either excessive inflation or high levels of unemployment. But the onset of stagflation during the 1970s—the simultaneous increase in both inflation and unemployment—was something never seen before and thereby put Keynesianism into question. A search began for new theories better suited to explaining stagflation and in turn new policies more effective in eliminating it. To some people, neoliberalism seemed to promise both. It argued that large welfare states and the high taxes necessary for sustaining them helped spur inflation because employers passed these costs along to consumers in the form of higher prices. Moreover, welfare states and taxes were said to have undermined the work ethic, crippled productivity growth, and stifled private investment, thereby jeopardizing economic competitiveness. Excessive government regulation of the economy was also targeted as a barrier to more robust capital investment and growth. The policy implications of all this were clear: governments should cut spending, taxes, and regulations if they wanted to cure stagflation.[19]

The neoliberal mantra diffused across developed and developing countries alike although in varying degree—depending partly on the strength of organized labor and on whether the left or the right controlled government. Nevertheless, within the advanced capitalist countries, neoliberalism and its backers were powerful enough to move the thinking of both center-left and center-right political parties farther to the right.[20] It also captured the collective imagination of professional economists, primarily in the United States and Britain, who then helped spread it around the world, initially to Latin America but then to Eastern Europe and Russia after the collapse of communism in the 1990s.[21] Particularly infamous were conservative economists from the University of Chicago—the so-called Chicago Boys—who served during the 1970s as advisors to the Pinochet government in Chile after a bloody coup ousted Salvador Allende's socialist government. And insofar as these economists staffed or advised organizations like the International Monetary Fund, the US Treasury, and Wall Street investment banks, which mobilized to open capital markets and national economies around the world to foreign investment, the so-called Washington Consensus emerged as an international variant of neoliberalism that pressured governments in the developing world to pursue neoliberal policies in exchange for financial assistance. Ironically, where neoliberalism led to the easing of capital controls, it sowed the seeds for severe fiscal and debt crises later on, as these states became vulnerable to capital flight—a lesson learned the hard way in the 1980s and 1990s in various Latin American countries, notably Brazil, Argentina, and Mexico as well as in Indonesia, Malaysia, and other Pacific rim countries.[22]

---

[19]Campbell (2004), chap. 5; Mudge (2008).
[20]Mudge (2011).
[21]Dezalay and Garth (2002); Fourcade-Gourinchas and Babb (2002); Fourcade-Gourinchas (2006).
[22]Wade and Veneroso (1998a, 1998b).

Continuities

Not all the changes we have discussed have been completely realized. Some states that possessed nuclear capacity did not seek to gain nuclear weapons, in part because they accepted the logic described above—that possessing a few weapons might be dangerous in a tense situation, encouraging an enemy to launch first if it feared that a strike on its own country might be necessitated by the possession only of first-strike capacity. Others have seen the matter differently. It is not irrational for a state to possess nuclear weapons if it makes it utterly clear to a power likely to intervene that they might then be used. The United States has not intervened in North Korea but did so in Iraq; Iran's desire to gain nuclear weapons results from understanding this situation. For another, the move away from the possession of territory toward the creation of greater human capital is not accepted everywhere. The most obvious exception is that of Putin's Russia, determined to dominate the Caucasus, able to annex Crimea, and perhaps to permanently destabilize Ukraine, whatever the cost both in terms of international opprobrium and of its own economic future.[23] Such considerations suggest continuities in the world polity; we now turn systematically to structures and practices that have remained largely the same in the contemporary world.

Structural conditions lurking in the background should not be forgotten. There remains an enormous difference in state capacities between the North and the South. States have long genealogies in the advanced world, and they are backed by wealth and by the creation—at best because of time, at worst because of violence—of cohesive national sentiment.[24] This is the world of successful nation-states in the North. In contrast, such success is not as prevalent or uniform in the South. Many states in the South are much newer, two centuries old in Latin America it is true but much more recent in Africa. Further, state capacity in the South is often limited by dependence and by poverty and by the difficulties created by the need to build shared national sentiment out of the diverse ethnic groups caged within the straight borders created by imperial powers. Analysis of such huge contrasting differences will be at the center of our attention later. But let us turn now to more immediate considerations.

To begin with, war has not completely lost its normal character, namely that of large-scale mobilization warfare between states. Perhaps, most striking was the long and bloody war between Saddam Hussein's Iraq and revolutionary Iran, in which more than a million people died. Traditional in a rather different sense have been the conflicts between India and Pakistan, most notably because one such engagement resulted in a successful secession—that is, the creation of Bangladesh, born from the ruins of East Pakistan. India and Pakistan remain at odds, of course, not least given continuing tensions in Kashmir. The relationship between the two states is toxic, with both interfering in

---

[23]There is a measure of complexity here. Realism should have made the United States and the EU sensitive to the desire of great powers—including the United States!—to have a measure of control or influence over territories close to their borders. More might have been gained by seeking for less.

[24]Lange (2015).

Afghanistan in order to weaken the other. The fact that both now have nuclear weapons makes this one of the most troubling regions in the modern world. The situation in the Middle East is perhaps even worse in that it is much harder to imagine solutions, in fact available in theory, being implemented. Israel and its neighboring states remain ready to fight, as they have done on three occasions in the postwar world, with the fear of Iran gaining nuclear weapons suggesting to some in Israel the wisdom of preemptive action. The possibility of conflict is the basic condition that explains the powerful role of the military in Arab states, a dreadful structural constraint on the possibility of liberal decompression and democratization—as we have seen recently in Egypt where a military coup ousted its duly elected president, Mohamed Morsi. Beyond these two hot spots stand others, past and present: tensions between India and China; the lack of resolution of the situation in the Malvinas/Falkland islands; and, perhaps most importantly, the new militancy of China in its near abroad—a development that has led the United States to engage in traditional balancing through its shift to Asia, and Japan to potentially revert to a more aggressive form of nationalism.

Let us turn from inter-state affairs to the national question. There are two obvious senses in which nationalism has most certainly not lost its bite in today's world. First, it may be that the presence of nuclear weapons has diminished geopolitical violence, but state competition abides in economic affairs. The speed of economic change has led some to speak of the need for "competition states," able to act flexibly and fast so as to swim successfully in the larger sea of global capitalism.[25] What is involved here is not just comparative advantage, based on cheap labor or particularly favorable demographics— for these factors can go quickly, as is already true demographically in the case of China whose recent fabulous growth rates accordingly look set to decline. What is required in addition to flexible political-economic institutions is, as noted earlier, the creation of human capital. This is far from easy, requiring high levels of education and a great reservoir of social legitimacy, often linked to appeals to national pride. In this regard, it is worth mentioning that nation-states are increasingly trying to bolster their economic competitiveness by branding themselves in order to attract investment capital—an appeal to nationalism of a sort. One need only watch European television or read European newspapers to see numerous examples of countries—from Qatar and Egypt, to Kazakhstan and Georgia—advertising their hospitable investment climates.

Second, just as important as economic competition between nation-states is the struggle to create national identity in the first place. The potential for conflict here is very great. The sociologist Matthew Lange has shown that a newly educated majority can seek to take the place of a dominant minority in ways that result in vicious ethnic conflict, as has most recently been seen in Sri Lanka.[26] The situation of African states, noted a moment ago, highlights the difficulties of nation building. Another worry is as yet muted, but it is possessed of genuinely radical potential. Rising states may yet

---

[25]Pedersen (2011).
[26]Lange (2013).

feel pressures internally, from newly confident educated sectors, wanting their state to play a more active part in the world. In authoritarian states, the temptation may exist to retain legitimacy by playing the national card—as in part happened in the great powers at the end of the nineteenth century. Of course, problems of strident nationalism are not necessarily restricted to the developing world, as is immediately apparent when one thinks of France, Denmark, Britain, and Switzerland. Nativist movements in these countries—particularly vocal recently regarding immigration issues—may yet disrupt the smooth workings of the European economy.

Another important continuity that links today's and yesterday's worlds is simply and bluntly that of inequalities of power within the world. While those living in the North often fail to realize the foundations of the world in which they live, states in the South do not suffer from a similar blindness. One obvious way in which this is so concerns the nature of international institutions. Rising states in the South have shown themselves in recent years to be deeply irritated by their lack of representation in such key institutions as the International Monetary Fund and the World Bank—and of course on the Security Council of the United Nations. And this is not just a matter of personnel: there is great resentment in the South toward policies that seem to protect the core of capitalism rather than to encourage development.

Much more important, however, is, as already noted in part, the power exercised by the United States. The United States has taken full advantage of its possession of the leading edge of power since the 1970s. The excess capital of the world has, after all, flowed to the United States to maintain its high standard of living rather than, as hegemonic stability theory would suggest, to aid in development elsewhere. One might take indebtedness as a sign of weakness, but then one might see it as something rather different—an extraction from other national economies made all the more attractive given the hegemon's ability to diminish its debt by printing money. This has had negative effects both on its allies and on emerging markets. One is tempted at times to describe such behavior as predatory, but it is perhaps best to diminish emotions by continuing to speak of seigniorage. Still, one can often usefully replace the term hegemony with that of empire insofar as the key decisions of the North are taken in Washington. For another side of American power is geopolitical. The United States has been involved in military action throughout the world in the postwar period, most recently fighting the longest wars in its history in Iraq and Afghanistan. It is worth characterizing the situation of the United States in terms of the categories developed to this point. The United States is at least as much a heroic as it is a trading state. Symbols of its heroic capacities abound, from the fact that it has military facilities in about a third of countries in the world to the realization that its own military expenditures account for roughly half of total military expenditures world-wide, with its spending equaling that of the next seven powers combined.[27]

---

[27]U.S. Department of Defense (2013), p. 7.

It is important too to note that not all nation-states succumbed to neoliberalism. Political economies, particularly in the advanced countries, did not embark on wholesale institutional reform. Despite the fact that corporatist bargaining was decentralized in some countries, it was not abandoned nor were welfare states dismantled, even if some were scaled back—and regulatory reform was often more a matter of reregulation than deregulation.[28] Furthermore, East Asian countries such as Japan, South Korea, and Singapore continued to pursue developmental policies where the state played a major role in guiding industrial development and innovation by means of extensive bureaucratic structures, tight state-industry linkages, and public-private innovation alliances. This was not a matter of state planning but rather what Richard Samuels called the "politics of reciprocal consent" in which business leaders, politicians, and state bureaucrats came to agreement on how each will proceed in the collective pursuit of national economic competitiveness.[29] Something similar was going on in other developing countries, not least in India where politicians, civil servants, and business leaders were neither overly cozy nor so far removed from each other as to undermine constructive dialogue and innovation—a situation referred to by Peter Evans as "embedded autonomy."[30] Thus, contrary to those who have argued that nation-states are being hollowed out, weakened, or otherwise emasculated as a result of globalization and the rise of neoliberalism, we still see a wide variety of nation-states and political economies in the world today.

A final consideration is necessary even though it might seem to contradict much that has already been said. Bluntly, surprises are of the very essence of world politics. What was wrong with Francis Fukuyama's celebrated declaration that history had come to an end was not the particular points he made about world politics, about which he was often insightful, but the naïve belief that a smooth and homogeneous world order had been created. We can see immediately that this is not so. Such surprises come in two forms, positive and negative.

An example that might at first glance seem positive is that of the revolution in energy supply resulting from fracking, the accessing of underground oil and gas supplies hitherto out of reach of standard technologies. There is now pressure in the United States, increasingly self-sufficient in energy once again, for rules to be changed to allow for the export of oil. This development may have three enormous consequences. First, there is no longer any justification for heroic policies toward the rest of the world based on the view that supplies of oil have to be protected. However, this does not rule out entirely heroic action for America. Even if maintaining access to foreign oil supplies is less of an imperative nowadays, the United States still feels that it has interests in promoting security in the Middle East—above all, through the prevention of nuclear proliferation. Second, this huge energy bonanza has the capacity to markedly improve the economic situation of the United States: large numbers of jobs are already being

---

[28]Swank (2002); Vogel (1996).
[29]Samuels (1987).
[30]Evans (1995).

created, while the costs of actual production has already been so much lowered as to create a significant advantage over rival states within the advanced world. But, finally, there may be a serious downside to this development, justifying the qualification in the opening sentence of this paragraph. Climate change poses a fundamental challenge, we argue later, for the future of the world. The technological sophistication involved in fracking is exactly what is not needed insofar as it diminishes the attention that should be given to sustainable development.

Some of the negative surprises of recent years are obvious. One was the Organization of Petroleum Exporting Countries (OPEC) oil embargo in 1973 where several Middle Eastern oil producing countries refused to sell oil to the United States and a few other Western countries because the Americans had backed Israel militarily when earlier that year Egypt and Syria attacked it in an attempt to regain territory lost to Israel in the 1967 war. The price of oil quadrupled in a matter of months triggering stagflation in much of the West. The Iranian revolution sparked another hike in oil prices in 1979. The terrorist attacks in New York and Washington on September 11, 2001, immediately come to mind as another negative surprise.

Conclusion

Our analysis is largely in line with that offered by Michael Mann at the end of his great philosophical history of power.[31] The central features of our world are threefold. First, capitalism now reaches the whole world. All states are deeply engaged in striving for national economic competitiveness. Their engagement involves all sorts of industrial policies, particularly among the emergent powers of the South—countries whose political formations are perhaps best described as developmental states. This is economic globalization today. The result can be neatly encapsulated by saying that Adam Smith now rules the world.

Second, globalization is far from being only an economic matter. The idea of the nation-state has been globalized. This means that competition between states is geopolitical as well as economic. The fact that countries spy on each other is then historically normal. But it is very important to stress that nation-state building is not complete everywhere. Many borders on maps have yet to be filled in with vibrant national sentiments. This matters in many ways, one of which concerns the external rule of Adam Smith. For a country to swim in that larger sea, it needs strong national self-organization. Many countries lack this capacity.

Finally, we query the ideal typical statement about capitalism—that it has no state to command it—because the United States has used its hegemonic power to attempt this. The imperial pretensions of the United States may seem strange by historical comparison, though not because it refuses to admit that it is an empire—for that

---

[31]Mann (2014).

was also true of the British. Rather, its empire is essentially non-territorial, with few being prepared to die for it. Nonetheless, American power remains so formidable that globalization can sometimes best be seen as Americanization. Henry Ford once quipped that customers could buy a Ford automobile in any color they liked as long as it was black. The same might be said about American foreign policy: all countries should be allowed to choose their own way, as long as it is the American way.

CHAPTER 3
CHALLENGERS?

Perhaps the single most important issue in the postwar world has been that of development, of polities determined to catch up with the advanced North—an aim that became imaginable with the rise of Japan, the first Asian industrial power. This chapter pays especial attention to the BRICs given the contemporary claim that they may overturn the current ordering of the world political economy. The acronym is unfortunate for several reasons. The four countries exhibit tremendous variation in the ways in which they have managed the issues of security, order, and national belonging. Furthermore, their interests do not always neatly overlap. Then some argue that the EU is quite as much a challenger to the United States; we consider this issue in Chapter 5. Finally, if Russia is scarcely a rising power in economic terms, as we will argue, there can be no doubt about its desire to challenge the United States geopolitically. But we begin by noting the two approaches that dominated development theory until recently. Immediate characterization of these positions will allow our own approach, in this chapter and the next, to become clear.

The nature of development

The initial postwar expectation was that decolonization would lead seamlessly to economic and political development. Such "modernization theory" suggested that urbanization, a more extensive division of labor, and social mobility would lead to the adoption of such Western values as dedication to work, materialism, individual achievement, and progress in science and technology. The logic of industrialism would eventually cause the economic, political, and cultural systems of these societies to resemble those in the advanced capitalist world, although the routes taken by different societies were not likely to be the same.[1]

Key theorists of this school were far from naïve, stressing that the social changes involved would most likely be achieved from above, from a state determined to drag a recalcitrant society into a new world. This meant that forced development might rule out democracy. Creating an educational system typically requires a decision as to which language should be used in society. In Algeria this meant Arabic, given that a war had just been fought against the French and the fact that Berber was at that time

---

[1]Kerr et al. (1960).

a low rather than a high culture. Such a decision of course requires social engineering, the suppression or loss of some identities, and the creation of a new one. Exactly the same point must be made about industrialization. Peasants move from the country to the city, in part through attraction but often quite as much because of government policies determined to provide labor for the infant industries they seek to build. The changes involved are so total that democratic control is almost a contradiction in terms.[2] Crucially, the first fruits of development must not be spent: primitive accumulation effectively involves seizing the surplus created by the incoming generation of factory workers for investment purposes.[3] Development is painful, as is utterly obvious to anyone who has lived outside the advanced world. Countries seeking to make the transition to the modern era very often have pictures of their leaders, Moses of their countries, in every classroom—perfectly symbolizing the centralization of power that is involved. But the theorists in question did not lack hope. The creation of a complex society was likely in the longer run to create pressures for political change. Forced development might rule out democracy but it would bring liberalization in its wake, perhaps opening the possibility for democratization later.

In the alternative approach, economic growth and prosperity let alone democracy were not natural corollaries of political independence. To the contrary, the great industries of the advanced world were seen by such "dependency theorists" as the Brazilian intellectual Henrique Cardoso as likely to so flood the economies of the South as to reduce them to perpetual weakness, merely the source of raw materials and cheap labor for the more advanced capitalist countries—with the added insistence that an element of the local elite, a comprador bourgeoisie, would benefit from this exploitive situation and to some extent oversee it.[4] The extraction of vast amounts of wealth from Chilean copper mines during the 1960s and 1970s by multinational corporations in the North is a classic example. In short, dependency would be more or less everlasting as long as the South remained under the political and economic thumb of the North.

The two approaches do agree on some points, notably in stressing that states need to organize their economies, not least by protecting their infant industries. Further, both theories draw our attention to certain empirical realities—with both equally being in error as well. Where exactly do we stand?

If a competition had to be held between the two theories, modernization theory would have to be declared the winner. For development has taken place, and it is taking place now in such a way as to possibly affect the balance of power in the world. It is abundantly clear that state power has played crucial roles in successful modernization. The success of the challengers is not a story about unfettered markets but rather one of many states intervening in markets in various ways and with positive effects. South

---

[2]Gellner (1967).

[3]Kohli (2004).

[4]One should remember that the position is far from new. Alexander Hamilton had argued in 1813 for the protection of nascent American industry in his "Report on Manufactures", and his views received systematic exposition in Friedrich List's *System of National Economy*. Amin (1976); Baran (1957).

Korea is a prime example of a developmental state—that is, of a state able to mobilize protectionism, finance, and a host of other administrative and policy tools to guide industrialization in rather successful ways, particularly when done in cooperation with key actors in civil society who provided information about the needs of the economy that was useful to policymakers—an "embedded autonomy" of the state within society allowing a "coercive-capitalist" route to modernity.[5]

It is important to note that this success story should not be used as the basis for much in the way of generalization because conjunctural factors were very much part of this social formation. First, Japanese rule over South Korea was direct rather than indirect: the viciousness involved cannot be denied but neither can the increase in state capacity nor the fundamental land reform pushed through by the Japanese. Second, South Korea had large injections of American capital, given for geopolitical rather than economic reasons—as was true of other countries the United States considered to be strategically important, a category that, importantly, did not include Latin America. Third, the state benefited from intelligent policy. There is a crucial difference between "import substituting policies" designed to protect infant industries that last and those that are temporary.[6] The former have often been catastrophic, creating powerful vested interests that maintained an industrial structure that became aged and ever more costly for the society it was designed to serve, as was true until very recently of India's steel industry. The alternative approach has had considerable success, notably in the South Korean cases of Hyundai and Samsung, where limited-duration tariffs hastened upgrading and innovation and where protective measures were tied to export obligations—strategies learned in part from the Japanese success twenty years earlier in autos, steel, and consumer electronics.[7] Finally, all of this was probably dependent on prior national homogeneity, with the national cohesion of South Korea being greatly enhanced by anti-communist feeling consequent on the division of the Korean peninsula.[8] Nonetheless, the South Korean success story does nothing less than confirm the hopes of modernization theory. For, political liberalization did follow a surprisingly able authoritarianism with the creation of a more diverse and contentious society, such that democracy is now consolidated in this South Asian country.

But the centralization of power has not always worked in this benign and beneficent way. The "authoritarian high modernism" identified by James Scott has caused enormous suffering—and it has, still more importantly, often massively set back economic development.[9] Russia was one of the world's great grain exporters in 1914. But collectivization so ruined Russian agriculture that it is now dependent

---

[5]In this regard, developmental state theories trump modernization theory (e.g., Evans 1995; Guillén 2001; Samuels 1987; Weiss 1998).

[6]Hall and Zhao (1994).

[7]Weiss (1998), pp. 73–74, (2003), p. 252.

[8]Janelli (1993). Kohli's excellent (2004) book neglects this; indeed he is oddly blind to the significance of the national factor.

[9]Scott (1998).

on the outside world for its supply of food. This suggests that the slow pace of development in both India and Brazil resulting from democratic pressure may be less a catastrophe than an advantage, given the long-term benefits of the politics of checks and balances. And an important consideration can be added to this. Political decompression is never easy to achieve. Highly centralized polities, especially of socialist hue, tend to destroy civil society because of their fear that self-organization can be turned against the regime. In the Russian case, liberalization failed in large part because the reforming elite had no organized groups with whom they could make bargains.[10] Further, sudden democratization can be dangerous, releasing pent-up pressures that make consolidating any political opening almost impossible, as was true in Russia after 1989 and in Egypt in very recent years.[11] The Soviet Union collapsed in large part because nationalism stepped into the vacuum caused by state breakdown. The Chinese are well aware of this, as they are of the certain fact that socialist planning from above, bereft of any market forces, is but a dead end. They seek to reverse Gorbachov's policies by having *perestroika* before *glasnost*. The extent to which this will allow the creation of partners able to engage in some process of political decompression is one of the questions of the age. And one should beware of presuming that social evolution will necessarily lead to liberalization. Germany developed before 1914 from above, and it would likely have continued to grow effectively but for defeat in war. Both Russia and China are authoritarian great powers, and both look to be essentially stable.

But there is an important negative point to be made against modernization perspectives. Significant areas in the South are scarcely developing at all. We need to go a little beyond classical dependency theory to understand what is involved. The first wave of state building took place in the North and the second in South America—the world in which dependency theory was created. But the third wave of state building is largely African and wholly recent.[12] It makes little sense to talk of development in Africa being distorted so as to accommodate the industries of the North. Rather, the North as a whole has recently tended to ignore this huge continent, whose disappearance off the face of the globe would have not had a major impact on the workings of the world economy. Hence, the understanding of weak states, which modernization theory has trouble explaining, must involve variables that are not just socioeconomic in character—above all, those concerned with ethnic divisions.

The contrast between success and failure is overdone, and we do not in fact hold to a dichotomous either/or view of the state of development theory. The next chapter makes this explicit, noting that the weakness of African states is not absolute before considering a handful of states that occupy, so to speak, middling positions, allowing

---

[10]Bova (1991). With hindsight, the claim made by Kirkpatrick (1979)—that state socialism, unlike authoritarian capitalism, could not be liberalized—seems justified, despite the opprobrium it caused at the time.
[11]Snyder (2000).
[12]Lange (2015).

them more or less to muddle through to greater development of one sort or another. This chapter will show that the BRICs have continuing weaknesses despite their undoubted advance. And we should be careful not to read too much into their advance in any case, for it anyway rests on conjunctural factors. All of the BRICs are continental powers blessed with huge resources and therefore scarcely to be compared with the large number of smaller states in the South. Further, these countries—even India—were never reconstructed by imperial powers as was true, for instance, of many West African states. One can risk a generalization: successful development seems to rest on a measure of linkage to historic institutions and patterns; *tabula rasas* present more obstacles than opportunities.

The BRICs

We are skeptical about the threat supposedly posed by newly rising powers. A first skeptical consideration concerns the nature of threat itself. It takes but a moment to realize that the height of threat comes when one wishes to assail a genuine enemy, either because one has something superior to offer or because the very presence of the enemy makes one's own existence completely precarious. The vital consideration that follows from this is that threats in the contemporary world are nothing like as great as they were in the immediate postwar period. The maximal moment of threat from the Soviet Union probably came in the early interwar years, when its ideological thrust against capitalism was filled with enthusiasm and belief.[13] The ideological threat has of course now disappeared into thin air. The nuclear threat has diminished somewhat as well. A similar story can be told about China. Some of the extreme statements of Chairman Mao were viscerally oppositional in character, hoping that popular movements would destroy states altogether and even contemplating the possibility of nuclear war on the grounds that China would survive it, blessed as it was by its huge population. But the 1970s witnessed the end of this radicalism, first in coming to terms with the United States and then in moving away from economic autarchy to trading with the rest of the world. China may not be happy within the current ordering of world politics, but it is seeking to change the rules rather than to destroy the system. All of this can be summarized in the simplest way. War is no longer a preferred option, not least as there is much more general awareness of the costs that the most recent military revolutions impose.

A second reason for skepticism, discussed in Chapter 2, is that a sea change in political economy has to a large extent taken place. Military conquest is no longer seen

---

[13]Threats, of course, ebb and flow. A key problem of the interwar period was the reluctance of Western powers to ally with the Soviet Union, thereby making balance of power politics in Europe difficult if not impossible. Some real sense of threat was present too after World War II, although one suspects that traditional geopolitical concerns had as much to do with this as did fear of a rampant ideology—particularly insofar as nuclear weapons were involved.

as a prerequisite for growth and development—a recognition that gives the rising powers a measure of confidence that they can be part of a world polity that no longer threatens them. The costs of holding territory in the face of nationalist movements typically far outweigh all benefits. Just as important, however, is the realization that the advanced powers can gain much that they need in the world economy through different means. FDI, the mobility of knowledge and capital, inter-firm alliances, and joint ventures can bring crucial benefits through cooperation. In today's world, attempting to capture these benefits by occupying new territory is likely not only to be expensive but to fail.

Third, rising powers have further reasons for confidence in the world polity. On the one hand, the norm of non-intervention together with great reluctance to change territorial boundaries gives a measure of security lacking before 1945. On the other hand, the world economy is not so closed that the newly rising powers have no chance of entering into it. In this regard, it is very important to note that there is a web of institutions into which rising powers can be and have been introduced—often with assistance from the United States and others in the North. Of course, some seats at the table have greater centrality than others, above all in the United Nations Security Council, but once again one observes struggles to change rules—to have the next head of the IMF, for example, come from the South rather than from Europe—rather than to disrupt the existing system as a whole. Still, the embrace of institutions like the WTO or the G20 has the capacity to de-radicalize rising powers. Brilliant research by the sociologist Kristen Hopewell deserves special consideration here for it shows that not everything goes in one direction. Brazilian agribusiness was able to mount successful campaigns against the subsidies given to sugar and cotton by the EU and the United States, respectively, using the tools created by the North against them! Her research is interesting in another way: the ability of Brazilian agribusiness to thrive in an open international market puts it at odds, despite much rhetorical cover, with India and with many weak states.[14]

The fourth factor concerns the changing nature of elites within a more integrated world. In the late nineteenth century, elites often sought to advance by modernizing their societies through state and nation building. As noted above, this often involved visions of territorial conquest. An alternative is now open to some elements of elites in the South—to leave their societies behind and join the action elsewhere sometimes with the intent of staying abroad but sometimes with the intent of returning home. Immigration of elites from the South to the North to become better educated, to facilitate business deals, and for other reasons is becoming more commonplace. In 2012, nine of the top ten countries from which most immigrants left were in the South, and seven of the top ten countries to which they moved were in the North.[15]

---

[14]Hopewell (2013).

[15]http://peoplemov.in Accessed January 2014. The top ten emigration countries ranked include Mexico, India, Russia, China, Ukraine, Bangladesh, Pakistan, United Kingdom, Philippines, and Turkey. The top ten destination countries ranked include the United States, Russia, Germany, Saudi Arabia, Canada, United Kingdom, Spain, France, Australia, and India.

For example, China was the number one source country for immigration to Canada in 2012. The Canadian government issued 32,900 permanent resident visas as well as 25,245 study permits—an increase of 235 percent since 2004.[16] One reason why housing prices in Vancouver, British Columbia, have become outrageously expensive is the increased presence of rich Chinese willing to pay enormous amounts of money for real estate. Of course, elites from various Latin American countries including Brazil have been moving to the North for decades to study at universities and to cultivate economic and political connections with which to improve their lives and those of their fellow citizens.[17]

In sum, we see no fundamental challenge to the North from the newly rising powers of the South. This is not to say, however, that these countries can be ignored. As we noted in the previous chapter, the South's percentages of global trade as well as world FDI inflow is growing, the latter having exceeded 50 percent for the first time in 2012. The economic development of the BRICs has been impressive, and it has at times been based on a new form of multinational enterprise—one that competes less on its brands and new products and more on managerial and organizational skills, logistics, flexibility, learning, and efficiency.[18] Table 3.1 shows that since 1999, the BRICs have established much stronger records of GDP growth than key countries in the North. This has continued for the post–2008 financial crisis era. Indeed, since 1980, annual GDP growth rates among the BRICs surpassed the G7 as well as the emerging markets

Table 3.1 Average annual GDP growth rates

	1994–1998	1999–2003	2004–2008	2009–2013
BRICs				
Brazil	−0.3	7.5	2.7	0.9
Russia	−7.8	4.5	4.3	3.4
India	8.5	10.5	6.3	3.2
China	9.2	10.4	9.3	7.8
Key Countries in the North				
Germany	−5.1	4.2	3.0	0.7
Japan	−5.5	4.7	−0.6	1.9
USA	−3.1	2.4	1.8	2.2

Source: World Bank (2013b).

[16]Citizen and Immigration Canada (2013).
[17]Babb (2001); Dezalay and Garth (2002).
[18]Guillén and García-Canal (2010), chaps. 1 and 2.

worldwide.[19] The BRICs are now the only trillion dollar economies outside the North. This is certainly due in part to the fact that China, India, and Russia are among the thirty countries that improved their regulatory environments the most, through simplifying construction permitting, easing the administrative burden of tax compliance, and protecting minority shareholders.[20] That said, Table 3.2 shows that for the most part they still lag behind the North in several measures of military and economic power as well as human capital. Similarly, Table 3.3 shows that the quality of their regulatory environments lags the North by considerable margins. Nevertheless, there is significant variation among them to which we now turn.

Table 3.2 Characteristics of the key Northern and Southern/BRIC countries, 2009

| | World | North | | | South (BRICs) | | | |
		USA	Japan	EU	Brazil	Russia	India	China
Military Characteristics								
Military expenditures, $billion	1,544	661	51	298	26	53	37	100
Nuclear warheads deployed	8,392	2,702	0	460	0	4,834	70	186
Economic Characteristics								
GDP, $billion PPPs	72,154	14,044	4,083	15,618	1,999	2,678	3,791	9,057
GDP, current $billion	58,078	14,044	5,033	16,347	1,594	1,222	1,381	4,991
Per capita GDP, current $ PPPs	10,668	45,745	32,006	31,192	10,344	18,878	3,281	6,803
Stock of outward FDI, $billion	18,982	4,303	741	9,006	158	249	77	230[a]
Income inequality, gini coefficient[b]	—	0.380	0.320	—	0.539	0.423	0.368	0.462
Human Capital Characteristics								
Internet users per 100 people	27.1	78.1	77.7	67.1	39.3	42.1	5.3	28.8
Literacy, % adults	83.7	99.0	99.0	99.5	90.0	99.5	61.0	95.9
Universities ranked in top 100	100	32	6	35	0	0	0	2[c]

[a]Excluding Hong Kong ($834bn).
[b]Most recent years available.
[c]Excluding Hong Kong (three universities).
Source: Guillén and Ontiveros (2012), pp. 91, 140–141.

---

[19]*The Economist* (2013a), p. 21. Weighted by share of GDP at purchasing-power parity.
[20]IBRD/World Bank (2012).

Table 3.3 Levels of clean government and business

	Public sector corruption		Regulatory environment			
	Rank	Score	Ease of doing business	Starting a business	Enforcing contracts	Trading across borders
BRICs						
Brazil	69	43	116	123	121	124
Russia	133	28	92	88	10	157
India	94	36	134	179	121	132
China	80	39	96	158	19	74
Key Countries in the North						
Germany	13	79	21	111	5	14
Japan	17	74	27	120	36	23
USA	19	73	4	20	11	22

Note: Public sector corruption data is from 2010 to 2011 and is based on 176 countries. Rank ranges from least to most corrupt (1 to 176); scores range from absolutely corrupt to clean (0 to 100). Doing business data is from 2013 and is based on 189 countries. Rank ranges from best to worst (1 to 189).

Sources: Public sector corruption data are from Transparency International, http://www.transparency.org/cpi2012/results (Accessed December 2013). Regulatory environment data are from The International Bank for Reconstruction and Development/World Bank, http://www.doingbusiness.org/rankings (Accessed December 2013).

Russia

The presence of Russia inside the group of newly rising powers is anomalous. Its economic growth rate plunged into negative numbers following the collapse of the Soviet Union. This was devastating in many ways to the population. In particular, one must remember the most basic fact of all when thinking about development, that of life expectancy. Only one industrial country has ever seen such a striking decline in life expectancy: vodka and unemployment reduced male life expectancy by more than ten years since the collapse of the Soviet Union. Although the country recovered in the 2000s, it still trailed both India and China economically until the 2008 financial crisis (see Table 3.1). Further, it is now experiencing serious difficulties. Table 3.3 shows that it is extremely corrupt compared to the other BRICs, although this seems to have translated into a more welcoming regulatory environment to business than that of the other BRICs. Vladimir Putin has demonstrated great skill in controlling the state and vanquishing his political rivals, thereby establishing somewhat of a personal autocracy, backed by an oligarchy which has taken to stashing vast amounts of money overseas in foreign banks, most notably of late in Greece. As Table 3.2 shows, it also leads the BRICs in outflows of foreign direct investment. The same table also indicates that despite the fortunes that have been amassed since the early 1990s, the Russian economy tends to lag the rest of the BRICs in terms of its size, except in terms of per capita GDP, and it does not even come close to countries in the North. One is hard pressed to identify many Russian products or services with the notable exception of oil and gas that are competitive in global markets today. Since the 2008 financial crisis, growth rates among all the BRICs have slowed considerably but less so in Russia than in the other countries, which suggests that at least in terms of finance, the Russian economy is less integrated with the international economy and therefore less exposed to its gyrations than the others.

Russia, of course, still enjoys residual benefits of its former superpower status. Its trump card is its nuclear arsenal (see Table 3.2). But as indicated earlier, the world has changed in ways that tend to neuter this sort of power. Of course, Russia still enjoys a seat on the UN Security Council and is a member of the G8 and G20 among other international organizations. Its geopolitical drives have destabilized the world in recent years. The backing of the Syrian government, despite Bashar al-Assad's use of chemical weapons against his own people in the civil war, with both financial and military assistance has helped prolong conflict within that country—and in doing so has contributed to instability in the Middle East. Russia has also remained an ally of the Iranian government further exacerbating troubles in the region. Its control over vast oil and gas reserves, reminiscent of other semi-peripheral countries, has given it leverage over some of its neighbors much to the chagrin of countries in the North. Ukraine rejected a trade deal with the EU in order to join a Russian dominated customs union with Belarus and Kazakhstan—a switch rumored to have been facilitated by Russia's promise to sell energy to Ukraine at discounted prices. Popular rebellion in the West of Ukraine, absurdly insensitive at the start to the fears of Russian ethics in the East, gave Putin the occasion to annex Crimea. The immediate future is very murky. National sentiment in Ukraine strengthened noticeably during 2014, with the nationality question in fact diminished by the loss of Crimea. Some sort of federal arrangement may yet allow for the maintenance of territorial integrity.

There is a sense in which all of this behavior is what one would expect—pure realism, helping those who are enemies of Russia's main rival. But if Russia remains a force to be reckoned with in geopolitical affairs, one wonders at the cost in terms of social and political development. The refusal to downsize, that is, to let Chechnya leave, will scarcely advance well being in the metropole. Any move to limit access to advanced markets is likely to curtail economic innovation, as the protestors in Kiev in 2014 so clearly realized. Behind everything is a question of identity. Is Russia to be a powerful nation-state or will it hang on to its historical identity as an imperial nation? To adapt Dean Acheson's comment about Britain, one can say that Russia has lost its empire and does not as yet know how to behave. Of course, it is not the case that progress is totally lacking when dealing with some nationalities in Russia's interior. But the insistence on controlling the near abroad distorts politics at home for no measurable economic gain. In terms of economic change within the world political economy, more consideration should be given to the other members of the BRIC group.

China

In the final analysis, it is change within China that makes talk of rising powers meaningful. Tables 3.1 and 3.2 show that China's growth rate has been extremely impressive, even after the 2008 financial crisis. China also has a nuclear weapons capability, albeit one considerably more limited than those of either Russia or the United States. Further, it holds a seat on the UN Security Council, thereby commanding a certain status in the geopolitical world. It is an important source of finance for other developing countries including those in Africa and Latin America. Finally, it differs markedly from Russia in having a history of greater national and linguistic homogeneity. This is not to deny the national questions that arise in Tibet, Hong Kong, Taiwan, and parts of Central Asia but merely to note that the sheer weight of China's population makes it unlikely that fundamental territorial change will occur. Nonetheless, what concerns us most is the growth of its economy.

Thanks to a number of reforms beginning in the late 1970s that decentralized political control of the economy and permitted citizens, regional and local governments, and state owned enterprises to participate in capitalist markets, China's economy has grown at an extraordinary pace. This has been helped further by the fact that China's regulatory environment for business has improved considerably and is now at least as good if not better than the other BRICs (see Table 3.3). In the early 1970s, its exports were a negligible fraction of the world's exports, but by 2012, they constituted 7.1 percent of that total—roughly 60 percent more than Japan and ten times more than Russia. China's imports skyrocketed even more, accounting for 19 percent of the world total by 2012.[21] Today, it is the world's second largest economy accounting for roughly 10 percent of world GDP. Its economy has been growing at roughly 10 percent annually in the two decades preceding the 2008 financial crisis. During this time, it has also run current account surpluses, which in 2012 was about $193 billion. Estimates suggest that Chinese GDP will overtake US GDP by about 2019.[22] Furthermore, China has expanding economic interests in Africa, the Middle East and, of course, the North. It is also an increasing source of aid and finance for other developing states.[23] Rapid economic growth has enabled China to increase its saving rate from 20 percent of disposable household income in the mid-1990s to over 30 percent in 2011. In turn, this has enabled China to invest abroad.[24] Its outward FDI in 2009 was $230 billion (see Table 3.2). And with its savings, China has also purchased significant amounts of foreign debt, including $1.3 trillion of US debt—the largest share held by any foreign country.

As a player in global affairs, China has shifted from a limited geopolitical profile two decades ago toward a more active one. For instance, it flexed its muscles by disrupting the Copenhagen climate conference in 2009 and more recently by cautiously working

---

[21]World Trade Organization (2013), table A17.
[22]Mann (2013), p. 272; The Economist (2013a); World Bank (2013a).
[23]Breslin (2013), p. 627.
[24]Barnett et al. (2012).

against American military intervention into Syria. Yet, China does not appear, as noted, to have any interest in overhauling the international governance system, which is not surprising because the Chinese have benefited from it economically.[25] It is actively embracing existing global norms and collaboration mechanisms. For instance, it adopted elements of international bankruptcy protocols following the 1997 Asian financial crisis.[26] It also promotes and defends the norm of state sovereignty including allowing countries to develop their own political and economic systems rather than having them imposed from without. Furthermore, it belongs to the WTO, IMF, and World Bank, where it has tried to increase representation of other developing countries and encourage fairness toward them. Put differently, it has called for the incremental reform—not the fundamental transformation—of these organizations. It has been active as well in bolstering regional cooperation within the South, such as through the Association of Southeast Asian Nations (ASEAN) and a number of other multilateral arrangements in the region. In these respects, China is trying to be a responsible Great Power in the world today.[27]

Despite these initiatives, China's international profile has been tarnished in several ways. One is its rather dismal record on human rights illustrated graphically by its infamous crackdown on demonstrators in Tiananmen Square in 1989 as well as its continued policies of Internet censorship, jailing dissidents, controlling organized religion, and more—all of which have been criticized by both other governments and by various international organizations. These problems, of course, stem from its single party authoritarian form of government, which is rather corrupt relative to the North (see Table 3.3). This is, however, a complex matter. The elite knows all-too-well what happened in the Soviet Union and is clearly determined to hold on to power and is not averse to puritanical purges to that end. At the international level, China's diplomatic record has been marred by showdowns with Vietnam, South Korea, and Japan; by border disputes with India; by its ties with corrupt and genocidal governments in Africa; and by an inability to curb North Korea's nuclear ambitions.[28] It is here that the greatest danger lies. The regime gains strength from national solidarity given lessening enthusiasm for communist ideology. But nationalism can run out of control. The quip made when the United States destroyed the Chinese Embassy in the last Balkan wars—"on day one people protest against the United States, on day two the same, but on day three they protest against their own government"—has an uncomfortable ring in current circumstances. Centralized authoritarianism concentrates discontent on the state, making such regimes curiously brittle.

Another blemish on China's record is the growing level of inequality that has accompanied its economic development. In 2012, the top 10 percent of the Chinese population pocketed nearly 60 percent of its national income—a level of inequality far

---

[25]Ikenberry (2008); Subramanian (2011).
[26]Halliday and Carruthers (2009).
[27]Breslin (2013).
[28]Guillén and Ontiveros (2012), pp. 135–136.

surpassing most OECD countries as well as many newly developing ones.[29] Table 3.1 shows that income inequality as measured by the gini coefficient is considerably higher than it is in the United States, which has higher levels of income inequality than nearly every country in the North. Inequality in China stems to a great degree from the vastly different economic possibilities found in rural and urban areas. So, despite its phenomenal rate of economic growth, China's average per capita income remains low—only about $6,800 in 2009 (see Table 3.2)—and it is estimated that 150 million people are living in what the UN defines as absolute poverty.[30] Given the potentially explosive political effects this could have internally, it is not surprising that the Chinese are trying to figure out how to build a welfare state that can cope with this problem.[31] Toward this end, they have recently sent delegations abroad to Scandinavia, Germany, and elsewhere to learn more about how other countries operate their welfare regimes.

China also faces problems at home that could dampen its economic prospects in the future. First, its university system is not strong and its telecommunications infrastructure pales in comparison to the North as well as to Brazil and Russia, at least judging by its low level of Internet access (see Table 3.2). This, however, may gradually resolve as the Chinese are working hard to improve their educational system, which Mao largely destroyed during the Cultural Revolution. Shangai's students were first in the world in math, science, and literacy on international exams in 2012.[32] Second, pollution and environmental degradation are rampant in China, which threatens not only its natural resources (e.g., wetlands, croplands, and forests) but also its human population as a result of human-induced disasters (e.g., invasive species, overgrazing, soil erosion, river flow cessation, salinization, and water and air pollution).[33] Third, to a considerable degree China's phenomenal growth has been facilitated by keeping its currency valued low relative to others in order to promote exports—a policy to which other countries, including the United States, have objected vehemently. All else being equal, if external pressure for revaluation succeeds, then one would expect a slowdown in China's growth rates.

Overall, it is hard to predict how things will turn out for China over the next few decades. Some believe that it is destined to become the world's major global power. Given the problems noted above, others are less sanguine, particularly because China does not have an ideology to export and because there are other very large newly developing countries in the world, notably India and Brazil, that can dilute China's relative economic and political influence. For instance, by 2030, China will be second to India in terms of population size—a population whose average age will get older, thanks to its one child per family fertility policy and therefore put demographic pressure on the Chinese state to

---

[29] *The Economist* (2012).
[30] Breslin (2013), p. 622.
[31] Lee (2007).
[32] *The New York Times* (2013).
[33] Guillén and Ontiveros (2012), p. 135.

shift resources away from development to welfare in order to maintain political stability at home. And the United States will remain substantially richer than China.[34]

Crucially, China does not seem to have moved up the value chain very far in terms of its productive capabilities. China adds, as noted, less than 5 percent to the value of Apple products, such as iPads and iPhones, made in that country.[35] Chinese firms do not have leading technologies or brands that are competitive in world markets. Nor will it be easy for them to acquire them as there is deep political and ideological resistance among Western governments to mergers and acquisitions of high-technology firms by large state-owned Chinese enterprises.[36] All these considerations can be encapsulated by noting that others have been trapped at the middle-income level. Cheap labor can produce an astonishing leap, but it may well not lead to sustained advance in technological innovation. As a result, we suspect that China will likely become a Great Power among others in a multipolar world rather than the preeminent power among all others.

India

India differs from China and Russia in that its political system is similar to that of many developed countries making it less likely that governments in the North will oppose mergers, acquisitions, joint ventures, and other cross-national business ventures with Indian companies. Most important, the character of its democracy is such as to diffuse conflict, rather than to concentrate it on the state. Bargaining of various sorts may have impeded speedy decisions, but popular control in the past prevented the famines that so scarred China.[37] In the coming years, democracy may well be seen to have considerable advantages, especially if China runs into severe difficulties as it tries to decompress its centralized polity.

India has particular achievements when dealing with different nationalities. India is a multinational federation of states, each of which has a dominant national culture and language. English is the colonial language and the international language of business. Hindi is the lingua franca of northern India, and an important language in movies, news broadcasts, and popular culture. English and Hindi are "link languages" spoken by many and used for business at the federal level and between the states and the federal government. Many states also have their own official language, such as Gujarati in Gujarat. As a result, most Indians speak the two link languages, if they come from a state where Hindi is the official state language. But many also speak one or two additional languages—that is, if their state language is not Hindi and if they belong to a linguistic minority within such a state. The important point is that multiple linguistic

---

[34]Breslin (2013) and Guillén and Ontiveros (2012), chap. 8 review the debate about China's future.
[35]Worstall (2011).
[36]Nolan (2012).
[37]Sen (1981).

competences have muted nationalist conflicts that might have occurred otherwise.[38] India still has occasional outbursts of nationalist violence at the communal level.[39] The outbreak that has mattered most in recent years took place in Gujarat, during the course of which many Muslims were killed. The state was then under the control of Narendra Modi who has since become the Prime Minister of India. Difficulties may now ensue. It was always the case that India had as a background unifying condition a majority of Hindus, and the Bharatiya Janata Party (BJP) that Modi represents has recently seemed sufficiently militant as to threaten the various accords that have ensured diversity in India.

India's economic performance in the 1990s was impressive judging from the fact that its rate of economic growth was comparable to China's. Even after the 2008 financial crisis, Indian growth rates were very respectable (see Table 3.1). Moreover, as Table 3.2 shows, its level of income inequality is much lower than that of its fellow BRICs. On the other hand, it remains a poor country judging by the size of its per capita GDP and high rate of illiteracy.

India's emergence as an important economic player on the world stage was driven to a considerable extent by concerns about China. Due to its military confrontations with China in the past as well as a recognition that China's economy was beginning to take off, Indian policymakers in the early 1990s started adopting an aggressive liberalization strategy to open up the economy. This began in 1991 with an almost 20 percent currency devaluation followed subsequently by several rounds of tariff reductions and more devaluations. At the time, India's peak tariff rate was 300 percent—the highest in the developing world—but by 1997, it had been lowered to about 20 percent. Liberalization also involved reductions in subsidies and tax incentives for export diversification, export processing zones, and a liberal foreign currency retention system. Policymakers also improved regulatory institutions and legal instruments to facilitate cross-national mergers and acquisitions. Although these reforms generated political opposition from social groups, labor, trade associations, nationalists, environmentalists, and intellectuals, India's leaders stuck to them over the course of several different governments, regardless of the parties in power, justifying them as a way to reverse the loss of competitiveness and respect vis-à-vis China and other East Asian countries. Put differently, policymakers invoked a globalist vision and legitimized it with nationalist rhetoric.[40]

Inspiration for these reforms came from three sources. First, policymakers realized that in order to counter potential Chinese aggression, India needed to beef up its own military capabilities, notably through the development of nuclear weapons, but that in order to do so it needed to bolster its economy. Second, policymakers borrowed many of their liberalization strategies from the Chinese, although Indian policymakers were

---

[38]Laitin (2008), pp. 88–92.
[39]*The Economist* (2013c).
[40]Alamgir (2003), p. 236.

able to implement them much faster than had the Chinese. Third, although reforms were guided from the top by national political elites, they did so in consultation with key economic actors. In particular, three major peak industry organizations meet regularly with the government leaders and inform them of what needs to be done in order to bolster India's competitiveness. Thus, in contrast to the 1970s and 1980s, where the state could not count on the private sector to provide it with information about which industrial policies would work or serve as an effective force for implementing these policies, things have changed and the Indian state now enjoys embedded autonomy—the situation where policymakers enjoy enough bureaucratic structure to avoid capture and clientelism but are not so far removed from civil society as to be out of touch with what it needs to develop and flourish economically.[41]

But like all the other BRICs, India has problems, which in this case could conceivably stunt its economic growth going forward. To begin with, India's electricity blackouts are legendary and water shortages are common. Its infrastructure is lackluster at best. Access to the Internet is extremely low and its literacy rate is much worse than the other BRICs, which is not surprising because it is also by far the poorest of the group (see Table 3.2). Moreover, corruption is high. Table 3.3 shows that India ranks 94th in the global corruption index and that the regulatory environment is considerably less friendly toward business than it is in the other BRICs. Things were so bad that in 2013 after years of trying, India's upper house of Parliament approved the creation of an anticorruption agency. Indeed, two key issues in recent elections were corruption and the need to cut red tape for business.[42] These are serious problems if India wants to continue to develop economically and ones that we suspect are related to India's federalist structure insofar as business regulations are likely to be inconsistent across state-level governments. In this regard it is important to note that the state bureaucracy as well as the government's own policies have prevented multinational corporations from developing operations in India to the extent that they would like.[43]

India occupies an ambiguous geopolitical position. It has nuclear weapons. It has refused to sign either the Nuclear Non-Proliferation Treaty or the Comprehensive Nuclear Test Ban Treaty, but it has cooperated with the International Atomic Energy Agency in other matters and has an impeccable record of nonproliferation. Like Brazil, India aspires to but does not yet sit on the UN Security Council. It is a democracy but sided frequently with the Soviet Union during the Cold War in part because the United States supported Pakistan. It has cooperated with the other BRICs to influence policy among the G20 and in the WTO but it has had one war (1959–1962) and persistent border disputes with China and competes with all the other BRICs for resources in Africa. Still, as India's economic power has been rising it has started to behave less cantankerously toward other nations, particularly the United States, and more

---

[41]Alamgir (2003), p. 242; Evans (1995).
[42]Harris (2013); *The Economist* (2013d).
[43]Narlikar (2013), p. 598.

responsibly as an emergent Great Power, not least through support for less developed countries in the WTO.[44]

In sum, India is trying to catch China economically, militarily, and diplomatically. Its population is nearly as large as China's and will soon be larger, although it suffers from a higher rate of illiteracy. Its growth rate has slipped recently and inflation is high. So, for the moment it is hard for us to envision India as a serious threat to the North.

Brazil

Brazil, the fifth largest country in the world by geographical area and by population, is the weak sister compared to China and India. During the 2000s, growth rates lagged behind the others most of the time (see Table 3.1). The size of its economy in terms of GDP is smaller, although it is doing significantly better on a per capita basis than India and China. Brazil also has by far the highest level of inequality of the BRICs, despite the fact that its inequality has been declining for the last 15 years (see Table 3.2).[45] It also has a regulatory environment that is not particularly friendly toward business (see Table 3.3). It spends less on its military than the others and is the only one without nuclear weapons. Its principal concern remains that of internal development, and there is a general awareness that external ambition might well produce a coalition of opposing powers.

On the positive side, however, its government is less corrupt than the others (see Table 3.3). And its population is relatively young with few people below the age of 20 and over the age of 60, which bodes well for its productivity going forward, particularly as it has a high literacy rate and, according to the OECD, as it is making impressive gains in improving its educational system.[46] It has also achieved macroeconomic stability, although its currency is soaring and thus restraining its international competitiveness. Large capital inflows have pumped up a bubble economy that could collapse if foreign investment races out of the country for some reason. Brazil suffered such a crisis in 1999 and accordingly has recently accused the United States of manipulating its currency at the expense of emerging markets. On a more positive note, Brazil has established a solid technological base in key industries, including automobiles, biofuels, and aerospace. It is also a strong exporter of dairy and other agricultural products, minerals, and oil (whose importance is growing in tandem with new offshore discoveries of vast reserves) and is a world leader in renewable energy production for automobiles, thanks to the government's ethanol policy of targeting sugarcane through subsidies rather than corn as the key source. Like the other BRICs, Brazil's economy is best characterized as state capitalism and includes two large state-owned multinational corporations.[47]

---

[44]Narlikar (2013).
[45]Centeno and Cohen (2010), pp. 165–166.
[46]*The New York Times* (2013).
[47]Guillén and Ontiveros (2012), pp. 15, 41, 60, 118.

During the early postwar era, Brazilian leaders were wedded to a developmental state model. But a military coup in 1963 and a purge of old elites in the late 1960s opened the door to a new breed of much more neoliberal economists—often US educated—who gradually gained prominence and eventually contributed to a counteroffensive against the junta, and this helped the return of civilian rule in 1985 that then established democratic institutions. After that debt crisis of the 1980s, the neoliberals pushed aside others who had long dominated the state. They now advise all the major political parties including those on the left.

However, Brazilian neoliberals had a deep appreciation for dependency theory so since the 1980s policymakers pushed a trade diversification strategy designed to reduce dependence on North American and EU markets. As a result, Brazil was a staunch supporter of Mercosur as well as opening up trade with Africa, particularly in construction, mining, and oil, which ramped up in the early 2000s with financial assistance from Brazil's National Bank for Economic and Social Development and various high value-added exports. In 1994, under the guidance of Finance Minister Fernando Henrique Cardoso, a plan was launched using judicious monetary policy, including currency devaluation in 1999, and other tools, such as trade liberalization, that finally curbed the hyperinflation and other economic problems that lingered since the days of military rule. This marked the launching of Brazil's impressive developmental trajectory into the twenty-first century.[48]

Brazil does not sit on the UN Security Council although it has aspirations in that direction. Moreover, Brazil has been doing so well economically over the last few decades and is so secure politically within the international system that it has little interest in any real change in the structure of that system. This is not to say, however, that Brazil lacks international vision. Its strategy, which was to cooperate with the North during Cardoso's presidency, pivoted under Lula's presidency during the 2000s. Now the idea is, firstly, to focus more on South–South relationships in order to assert itself as a regional power. In this way, the Lula administration has pushed Brazilian foreign policy to the left insofar as it advocates for its poorer neighbors while quietly continuing the center-right economic policies of his predecessor. And, secondly, insofar as North–South relations are concerned it seeks either to represent the interests of the South or to broker coalitions within the South thereby framing itself as a bridge builder between the two regions.[49] Remember though that the use of the WTO to further Brazilian agribusiness has not always been in the best interests of other developing countries. But that policy does indicate the presence both of economic muscle and of considerable state capacity.[50]

As such, although Brazil has made great strides in terms of development, it is not a threat or even a serious challenger to the North economically, militarily, politically,

---

[48]Burges (2013), p. 583; Dezalay and Garth (2002).
[49]Burges (2013).
[50]Hopewell (2013).

or ideologically. Indeed, one of its more important concerns at the moment is the competitive challenge it faces in places like Africa from China.[51]

Conclusion

All of the challengers we have discussed have been able to establish basic order in their societies. They have also been effective in establishing security of their borders. Brazil faces no particular external threats to begin with. India has built up its military capabilities, including nuclear ones, in response to worries about Pakistan and China. Neither China nor Russia face particularly serious threats either and in fact have both flexed their muscles of late—for China in the East China Sea where it is squabbling with Japan over a few small islands, and for Russia in the Crimea where troops have seized control of this region of Ukraine. In terms of national identity and belonging Brazil faces little in the way of nationalist disruption. India found political and institutional ways to contain whatever nationalist conflicts there might otherwise have been. China is largely homogeneous to begin with so with the exception of Tibet and parts of Central Asia does not have nationalist troubles at all. But Russia is wholly different, playing the irredentist card in Crimea and seeking to dominate its near abroad.

The point in all of this is simple: even in today's global economy states matter a great deal in shaping the developmental trajectories of their societies. What we find particularly interesting is how much variation there is in the role of the state among the emerging powers. China's state is based on single party rule espousing a modernized version of communist ideology that accepts to a considerable degree liberalization of its economy. In doing so the state has taken a strong role in decentralizing taxation to facilitate more efficient use of resources by lower levels of government; privatizing some but certainly not all of its state-owned enterprises; manipulating its currency in order to facilitate export-led growth; creating strong incentives to relocate people from rural to industrializing areas in order to man factories there; and supporting massive infrastructure programs, including the building of dams, railroads, and telecommunications systems. Meanwhile, Brazil and to a certain extent India have adopted more familiar developmental state models based entirely on capitalism but with more democratically organized governments. Russia's state has also played a forceful role in its postcommunist development, but it has done so with much more limited success. So, just as there is no one best practice among the advanced countries of the global North in terms of how states are organized and steer economic activity, the same is true among the rising powers.

---

[51]Burges (2013).

CHAPTER 4
STATES OF THE GLOBAL SOUTH

We have argued that a successful state provides order, security, and belonging, and as a result affluence to a society that controls it. Modern states of this type were created in Europe's Darwinian world, one that mandated fiscal extraction by means of bureaucratic development. The institutional state capacity that resulted was far from negative: it involved the provision of legal services, and the fostering and protection of economic activity—this being crucial since traders were mobile and prone to move (and thereby to increase the power of one's enemies) if they were treated badly. The endless interaction between competitive states and their societies had three dramatic consequences. First, there was further substantial institutional development. Second, distinctive national identities were created over time as diverse linguistic and ethnic groups merged into the culture of their states.[1] Finally, social forces reacted to the demands of their states for taxation and for conscription. The fight to control the state did much to enhance national identity, citizenship, and democracy. Third, this then led to substantial institutional development.[2]

It is now time to turn to the other side of the coin so as to look at the lack of success of states plagued by a mass of problems. Weak states have tremendous difficulty maintaining order within their borders, often because of an inability to cultivate a common sense of national identity and belonging. These states lack institutional capacity. They continue to live their half-lives, however, because of general observance of the norm of non-intervention. But our discussion does not stop here. Academic argument and political debate has concentrated, as noted, on the rising powers and failing states. We recognize both but insist that such dichotomous thinking is mistaken, failing to pay proper attention to the great variety in state and nation building within the developing world. Accordingly, we offer analysis, indicative rather than complete, of countries that are "muddling through," finding ways to advance without drawing great attention to themselves.

An anatomy of weakness

The weakness of a state, its inability to penetrate and organize its society, can best be measured through indices of political corruption, levels of fiscal extraction and measures of poverty, literacy, and development to which one can add analyses of the extent to

---

[1]Smith (1986).
[2]Mann (1993).

which ethnic groups are included or excluded from political power and share a sense of common national identity.[3] The extreme point of weakness can be seen in the presence of civil war, endemic violence, and head counts of refugees.

Distinctions need to be drawn, together with some understanding that weak capacities can ebb and flow.[4] Very few states have become so weak as to disappear, and even the weakest, such as Somalia, contain areas in which settled expectations survive. Analyzing degrees of weakness does not create analytic clarity, largely because different indices point in different directions. Zimbabwe is comparatively secure, but its polity and economy are now disastrous. In contrast, Iraq has recently been deeply insecure, despite relative affluence and some measure of welfare provision—which is not to say, a moment's reflection suggests, that it was entirely successful before the American invasion when ruled by Saddam's iron fist. Then it is clear that weakness can take different forms. Many sub-Saharan African countries are but lines drawn on the map, possessing "states" which scarcely deserve the name, often lacking much infrastructural reach and faced with a mass of competing ethnic groups. In contrast, Colombia has suffered because the FARC (Fuerzas Armadas Revolucionarias de Columbia) guerillas have been able to finance an insurgency through drug trafficking and kidnapping. Further confusion results when confronting the fact that interest in state weakness has sharpened because of al-Qaeda's attacks on New York. This has led to use of the term "failed states"—resisted here, as noted earlier, on the grounds that it is too self-centered, too much concerned with the effects of the weakness of others for us. In any case, many of the most miserable places in the world, from North Korea to the Democratic Republic of the Congo, and from Haiti to Myanmar, do not provide homes to international terrorists. Moreover, many of the terrorists in Iraq and Afghanistan are national rather than international in orientation. What may matter most to al-Qaeda are social networks, some of them in the West, rather than the presence of weak states. Still further distinctions need to be drawn. For one thing, it is a mistake to suggest that Muslim countries are weak: many Arab countries have this character, particularly in terms of low levels of literacy, unsustainably high levels of fertility, and political repressiveness, but this is not the case for all of them nor for Muslim countries outside the classical heartland of Islam.[5] For another, there is little correlation between weak states and disease—with South Africa suffering heavily from HIV/AIDS and Indonesia and Vietnam from bird flu. And a crucial consideration should be at the center of attention at all times. Bluntly, many weak states, perhaps especially in West Africa, are successful: they are predators, serving the few through exporting capital at the same time as they fail the many.

---

[3] Wimmer (2013).
[4] *The Economist* (2009). Cf. Rotberg (2003, 2004).
[5] Stepan and Robertson, (2003). Very varied comments can, of course, be made about different states. The United Arab Emirates and Qatar, for instance, are Arab states without low literacy rates and high birth rates; they are not as repressive as many of their neighbors—Qatar supported many of the Arab Spring uprisings; and their GDP per capita is at least as large as the leading West European nations (U.S. Central Intelligence Agency 2014). Pakistan is not really a weak state, as most of the country is under the state's control. But just as the state does not control the frontier provinces, nor does the president control all of the state.

Given these complexities, it makes sense to begin by noting four difficulties that latecomers face when seeking to establish states.[6] But a word of warning is in order. We should take care not to worship powerful states. Nazi Germany and Soviet Russia killed millions, and they collapsed in horror and ignominy. The point that will emerge from this is very important: one should not take for granted that copying the Western route to state formation is desirable.

First, geographical conditions hampered state construction in large areas of the world. This is especially true of sub-Saharan Africa.[7] The arid and tropical conditions of this region of the world sustained only small populations—often blessed, it should be noted, with the ability to move at will, so as to escape control. Much the same can be said about mountainous terrain: population density is again low, whilst the pastoralists of this world know how to fight as well as how to move.[8] Nepal, Pakistan, and Afghanistan have had difficulty in building states in these circumstances—as have countries in the Caucasus.

Second, economic resources can cause difficulties for state construction, albeit in directly opposed ways. On the one hand, several countries possess lootable resources, concentrated geographically and easy to trade outside the reach of the state. Blood diamonds is one such resource, drugs such as cocaine and opium another.[9] When non-state groups get their hands on these resources, they can challenge state power all-too-effectively. This was true in Sierra Leone in the 1990s, and it seems to be true in Afghanistan today—where drug monies allow insurgents to receive greater emoluments than do members of the regular armed forces. It is important, on the other hand, to remember that states require resources to gain salience. A poor society is unlikely to allow much state construction.[10] Just as importantly, states in this situation tend to buy allegiance by expanding state employment, often at the expense of the meritocratic norms essential to the establishment of powerful bureaucracies.

Third, latecomers face systematic difficulties when trying to create and strengthen their state structures. What matters most is the impact of imperialism. There was of course systematic difference in the British case between the Dominions and the areas of direct rule on the one hand and limited or indirect rule that applied much more extensively on the other. Metropoles sought to extract resources as cheaply as possible. Their administrative core was very small, with rule depending on patrimonialism and occasional coercion.[11] Incoherence and division characterized these puny Leviathans. Decolonization habitually did not leave pillars on which to build, merely varied sorts of vacuum.

---

[6]Lange (2010).
[7]Herbst (2000).
[8]Fearon and Laitin (2003).
[9]Snyder and Bhavnani (2005).
[10]Collier (2000).
[11]Corbridge et al. (2005).

Finally, state construction was hampered by the national question. For one thing, colonial rulers had no interest in creating a common national identity: their racism meant total exclusion of the native populations—which were often suspicious of and hostile to state structures thereafter. For another, imperialists often systematically worsened the situation through dividing so as better to rule. What was particularly damaging was the way in which the imperialists constructed ethnic identities, so as then to gain the support of one group against another.[12] Divide and rule strategies were enhanced by importing specialized middlemen—in the British case, South Asians into East Africa and the Caribbean. At worst, the legacy of such divisiveness led to horror, most obviously in recent years in the conflict between Hutus and Tutsis. Beyond this, however, is the deleterious effect that ethnic fractionalization has, in the eyes of most scholars, on economic performance—both through making it hard to reach common agreement and because a sustained sense of energetic cooperation and self-sacrifice is missing.[13] We have argued that exclusion is likely to radicalize. There is abundant evidence that this is so in weak states, very often leading to bids for secession with consequent escalations to civil war. Of course, all of this then makes it harder, through a negative feedback loop, to find the necessary resources for state construction.

These factors play out most strikingly amongst the understated, that is, the world habitually taken to include Haiti, East Timor, Nepal, Somalia, Afghanistan, Sudan, and a whole slew of West African states. Many of these countries have been marked by conflict, and about half return to this condition within 10 years of peace agreements. The international system has not been able to prevent these reversions. In the past 20 years, for example, $300 billion has been spent in Africa alone, yet the continent is still rife with regimes lacking the most basic infrastructural capacities—two million people a year are dying of AIDS, 3,000 children die every day of malaria, and 40 million receive no schooling at all.[14] The image that best conveys the reality of this world is of a leader in a capital city lacking the means to know what is happening in the rest of the country. In a sense, readers in the advanced world should not be too surprised by this picture. This lack of state capacity characterized their own states until rather late in the historical record, as basic exercises in fiscal sociology have demonstrated. But there is a difference. State capacities in the advanced world have in virtually every case expanded enormously over time, and they continue to do so as states become responsible for ever larger areas of public health and economic competitiveness. In contrast, many of the states mentioned in this paragraph have been going backwards, losing state capacity and infrastructural reach. Perhaps the classic instance is that of the Democratic Republic of the Congo, formerly Zaire, whose colonial transport infrastructure has now all but collapsed. Against this should be set the consideration already noted, namely that predatory regimes of this sort sometimes had sufficient capacity to find ingenious

---

[12]Mamdani (2001).
[13]Posner (2004a).
[14]Ghani and Lockhart (2008), p. 22.

ways to export capital for leaders and their entourages. The Zaire of Mobuto stands as the exemplar.

The character of this type of state derives from the nature of the postwar international order. The norm of non-intervention within the internal affairs of other states became a cornerstone of the world polity. What emerged in consequence were quasi-states, that is, states whose existence depended more upon international recognition than upon their own functional capacities for ruling their territories.[15] This norm was not imposed by the advanced world on late developing countries. To the contrary, the norm was adopted and maintained by the Organization of African States—which went so far as being prepared to condemn one of its own members, Julius Nyerere, for his part in bringing down the hideous regime of Idi Amin in Uganda. Such visceral attachment to the norm is fully comprehensible. Many African states have boundaries drawn up by colonial powers caring so little about pre-existing social groupings that their straight lines went through them. The "virtual reality" of boundaries places a premium on maintaining them. As every state is artificial, rectification or simplification would lead to generalized disaster.

The sinews of the state, everywhere and at all times, rest upon the ability to extract taxes from society. European states lived in such a competitive surround, as noted, that they were forced to dig into their societies: no one state could afford to sit still, thereby being bound to adopt any innovation, military, economic, and ideological, created by the leading edge of power so as to survive. The contrasting point about Africa—and, for rather different reasons, Latin America—is that militarized state competition has been avoided, ruled out by adherence to the international norm of non-intervention established in the United Nations shortly after World War II.[16] Capacities for fiscal extraction are accordingly low, with many states receiving a large portion of their monies from the outside in the form of aid. This limited interaction between states and societies has meant that citizenship politics have scarcely developed. After all, with limited taxation, citizens had no financial incentive to demand new rights in exchange. Just as important is the consequence of this fact for national identity formation. Ethnic and linguistic diversity in Europe blended into a singular national culture over time, for sure, but also as the result of shared struggle in war and of the horrible consequences that resulted. The diversity within African countries, often enhanced by the actions of imperialists, has not had to be diminished in a similar way. National identities most often have yet to be constructed.

If these background conditions gave Africa weak states, it is quite clear that state capacity weakened in many countries for long periods.[17] What matters most is a diminution in fiscal capacities, particularly in Africa. One reason for this is internal: single party rule very often led to the granting of monopoly powers that severely impaired

---

[15]Jackson (1990).
[16]Centeno (2002); Herbst (2000).
[17]Bates (2008).

economic development. But other reasons are external, notably the oil shock followed by the lessening of geopolitically motivated aid consequent on the ending of the Cold War. In these circumstances, states have become more militarized, with predation ever more likely to replace the rule of law.

This is not to deny that other factors are at work. Sheer poverty makes state building difficult. But a measure of caution and skepticism is in order here. The initial poverty of Vietnam did not prevent it developing, whilst the comparative wealth of Zimbabwe has not prevented its decline—with the different trajectories being best explained by the facilitating and predatory character of the states involved.[18] Equally, oil and diamonds do not in every case lead to state weakness. To the contrary, here too it is weakening of the state that allows rebels to seize such resources in the first place. Just as clearly ethnic conflict leading to civil war is often the result of a state's weakness, its inability to provide basic order in the face, on occasion, of mere teenagers armed with Kalashnikovs.[19] This is not to deny the ravages that resulted from conflict in Sierra Leone and Rwanda, and those that continue today in the Democratic Republic of the Congo. But the complex causal pattern deserves highlighting: poverty, the curse of lootable resources, and ethnic conflict result from weakness, which condition they then much exacerbate.

The depressing picture that has been derived from considering institutional weakness must be darkened still further by turning attention to the task that confronts latecomers, that of modernizing their societies. This is a careful formulation. The most immediate point to be made about the sorts of states with which this chapter is concerned is that they completely lack the capacity to force development in the way suggested by modernization theory. But it is very important to realize that the ideology involved, the belief that power should be centralized in order to foster development, was widely accepted. It provided justification for dictatorships which did little, except to prey on their own societies. And this brings us to the final point. Moments of democratization have often led to anarchy rather than to the consolidation of order.[20] Democratic openings often allow for the emergence and self-organization of highly undesirable groups—as has been the case with drug lords in Afghanistan in the wake of the defeat of the Taliban. The dilemma involved in this can be seen in the near schizophrenia of the viewpoint of one of the most important analysts of African states. The analytical passages of Robert Bates's book, *When Things Fell Apart*, making much of the dangers of democratization, of the emergence of undesirable groups and of the likelihood that the situation will spill out of control are followed by a despairing insistence that democratization must be undertaken on the grounds that some way must be found to control predatory regimes.[21]

The interim conclusion that suggests itself is that of the immense difficulties facing latecomer states. State power is needed, but very often the wrong type of state power—predatory rather than enabling—has been in evidence, doing more to

---

[18]Easterly (2008), p. 52.
[19]Laitin (2008), chap. 1.
[20]Posner (2004b).
[21]Bates (2008), pp. 108–20, 136–7.

prevent than to occasion development. This suggests the need for democracy, but sudden democratization can release forces that tear countries apart. One could go further. Consider just one example, the Zimbabwe of Robert Mugabe. A sensitive analysis by Mamdani begins by asking the question that facile moral condemnation so often obscures, namely how is it that his regime has lasted so long?[22] The most basic consideration is simply that the handover of power by Britain did nothing to deal with inequalities in land holding. Land redistribution was always likely to be popular, and it was politically needed given the presence of former guerilla fighters. The removal of groups brought in by the prior imperial power, Asians in Uganda as much as farmers in Zimbabwe, is comprehensible. There may be more of this, perhaps especially in South Africa.

There have been two notable policy responses in the West to the general picture that has been presented here. The American political scientist Jeffrey Herbst is utterly logical in following his analysis of the different paths of state formation in Europe and Africa with a brutal prescription—namely, that the norm of non-intervention should be abandoned, so that European style wars of consolidation, with all that implies for increases in solidarity, taxation, and citizenship, be countenanced and accepted in Africa.[23] In complete contrast, liberal humanitarians shocked by what they see on their television screens call ever more insistently for more intervention from the advanced world. One significant thinker, the Oxford economist Paul Collier, calls for military involvement so that local wars can be brought to an end, seeing in this a precondition of every other form of development.[24] A more limited position suggests that intervention can take the form of Western involvement in running weak states, a form of power-sharing between the weak and the strong.[25] These are dangerous counsels. If we look at the situation of exceptionally weak states from a different angle, in effect from the other end of the telescope, it will become apparent that they should not be accepted in light of the brutality and misery they often precipitate. Our starting point is simply that of recalling the horrors of occidental history. Appreciating the two areas of Western "vice" will make certain "virtues" of the rest stand out clearly. So, the counsels offered will be rejected on descriptive as much as prescriptive grounds.

The first crucial point to remember about the history of Europe in the twentieth century is that it has been incredibly bloody, with perhaps 70 million people killed and murdered in the course of population transfers, ethnic cleansing, and the Holocaust. The competition between states that had brought economic and social progress before the middle of the nineteenth century thereafter led to disaster. One reason for the change was simply the greater destructiveness caused once industrial means were applied to warfare. But still more important was, as argued, the way in which nationalism became linked to imperialism. The great powers came to feel that the possession of empires giving them

---

[22]Mamdani (2008).
[23]Herbst (2004).
[24]Collier (2000).
[25]Krasner (2005).

secure sources of supply and markets was necessary for their survival. Linked to this was the belief that national homogeneity was necessary for societal success. The areas of East and Central Europe in which national awakening came before state consolidation (that is, the areas in which diverse ethnicities had *not* blended into a single national culture) were necessarily affected by this belief—but so too were relatively homogeneous countries such as Germany, keen to remove the Jews and determined to cleanse Slavs from eastern territories conquered in war. The combination of these factors made Europe the dark continent of the modern world. The sad fact is that liberal democracy in the West rests in part on the back of the ethnic cleansing that took place. This should make us chary about presuming that our model of development should be recommended for others. Herbst is at least honest in acknowledging what was involved, but one still shudders to think of the deaths that would be involved were his advice to be followed.

A second equally important set of considerations about the West should be quite as much at the center of our attention. To begin with, one needs to be very cautious in recommending intervention, even though it may be necessary and desirable in extreme cases.[26] Troops welcomed initially often come to be seen, now that the nationalist principle structures world politics, as occupiers. Further, there is a dreadful tendency for those who recommend intervention not to think through the consequences of their policies. What matters about increasing hostility to the forces of intervention is that it puts up costs dramatically. There is very often a "disconnect" between the desire to help and the willingness to pay, whether in terms of money or lives. The institutions to sustain liberal interventionism are very weak. Intervention followed by retreat can be disastrous, as is the case with American involvement with the Muslim world in the last decade.[27] Two implicit, important points here need highlighting. First, Western institutions are not now somehow perfect; to the contrary, the lack of serious thought about foreign policy making, the inability to work out and to accept the consequences of state actions, is a key weakness. Second, states in the developing and underdeveloped world have sometimes been affected negatively because of the Western dominated structure of the world polity. This is obviously true of failed interventions, but it applies quite as much to neoliberal restructuring policies which often undermine attempts to develop state powers. And present circumstances make a further comment necessary. The failure of Western institutions, and the impact of that failure on the social world considered in this chapter, has a further element, namely the lack of order at the center of capitalist society.[28] For all the difficulties faced in the advanced West, it remains the case that the greater suffering will take place among the weakest in the non-European world.

If there is hope for the weak states, it will have to come internally by changing institutions in ways that help them better fulfill the requisite functions of order, security, and belonging. It is here that we wish to conclude properly, moving beyond the interim

---

[26]Easterly (2008).
[27]Rashid (2008).
[28]Reinhart and Rogoff (2008).

comments that have just been made. The situation of latecomer states is not necessarily hopeless, even if the road ahead for weak states is both dangerous and difficult. Against everything that has been said needs to be set the success of Africa in the last decade. Between 2005 and 2013, the continent overall has averaged an annual real GDP growth rate of 5.4 percent.[29] We can make the case with reference to Zambia—plagued by internal ethnic rivalries for many years, which had serious destabilizing consequences for that country. But when it managed to reform its political institutions, notably election laws, previously excluded ethnic groups were granted political voice and their political grievances diminished considerably. The country is now experiencing improvements in per capita income, school attendance, and life expectancy. Inequality and poverty remain high but between 2005 and 2013, real GDP growth improved averaging more than 6 percent annually.[30] This case reminds us of the limits of the term "failed states", thereby allowing us to end this section on a note of optimism.

Muddling through

One way to locate the middle range of states of the contemporary developing world is to begin by again looking at the proliferation of acronyms. One of the newest—MINT—draws our attention to Mexico, Indonesia, Nigeria, and Turkey, whilst recent discussion of the so-called "Next 11" adds Bangladesh, Egypt, Iran, Pakistan, South Korea, the Philippines, and Vietnam to the list of emerging countries. Further, the BRIC acronym is now often challenged on the grounds that it should include South Africa and Turkey. Before discussing some of these countries, it is worth insisting that the putative group to which they belong should not be seen as equivalent to the great continental powers discussed in the last chapter. It is very unlikely that these countries will have as large an impact on the world economy as China, Brazil, and India. These countries are much smaller, which also means that their potential challenge to the ordering of the world economy will be considerably smaller. Just as important, the world economy is now twice as large in real terms as it was in 1992; this too will mitigate the impact of these countries on the world economy.[31] Still, there will be development, taken by highly variable routes. Some routes are more democratic than others; some have more bureaucratic and less corrupt political institutions than others; some have more state ownership than others; some have more nationalist turmoil than others; and some are richer in natural resources than others. We introduce some exemplars of these different routes through consideration of three pairs, to which we add two comments.

South Africa's racial and ethnic divisions have long been the source of severe repression, poverty, inequality, and stunted economic growth. However, since the

---

[29]African Economic Outlook (2014).
[30]U.S. Central Intelligence Agency (2014).
[31]The Economist (2013a).

end of apartheid there was significant improvement. The African National Congress (ANC) has won all the elections since 1994 by a huge margin and still holds its share of the vote around 60 percent. During this time, the transition from white minority to black majority rule has been surprisingly smooth, thanks in part to Nelson Mandela's extraordinary role as the founding father of a new nation. The Truth and Reconciliation Commission also played some part in allowing past horrors to be put to one side, thereby allowing movement forward. There have been great strides in racial equality. For every black engineering student in 1994, there were 44 white students. Now their numbers are broadly equal. More than half of all blacks have bank accounts, compared with less than a fifth 20 years ago. Black professionals are still a minority, but a much larger one. Around 40 percent of senior managers are black compared with just 4 percent in 1994. Furthermore, annual economic growth rates have trended upward, peaking at around 5.5 percent prior to the 2008 financial crisis and now hovering around 2 percent. Moreover, the poverty rate declined from 41 percent in 1994 to 31 percent in 2013, exports as a percentage of GDP increased until the crisis, and inflows of FDI grew. A variety of social and infrastructure indicators also showed improvement, including average life expectancy, spending on education, and access to the Internet, cell phones, better housing, and freshwater. These improvements are attributable to South Africa's extensive mineral wealth, sound financial markets, infrastructure investments, and accelerating demand especially from the BRIC countries for South African exports. South Africa is the only African member of the G20.

Nevertheless, problems persist. Joblessness is rising rapidly as population grows. Unemployment is roughly 25 percent, excluding those who have given up looking for a job. Hence, South Africa still has extremely high inequality by world standards, sporting a gini coefficient of 0.63 in 2005 and has one of the highest poverty rates in the world. Life expectancy has actually fallen in the last two decades, mostly due to the disastrous lack of a serious HIV/AIDS policy during the presidency of Thabo Mbeki (1999–2008). Furthermore, despite recent efforts, the country still suffers serious infrastructural problems, notably chronic energy shortages. Political corruption is growing, especially within the ANC—not surprisingly given its domination of political life. The most recent example is the highly publicized $25 million expenditure of tax revenue on President Zuma's private home. Violent protests and strikes over lack of public services and corruption are frequent. Finally, even though the crime rate has fallen by half in the last two decades, South Africa still has one of the highest crime rates in the world. Its murder rate, for instance, is especially high—30.9 for every 100,000 people as compared with 4.7 in the United States.[32]

Still, these problems diminish in comparison to those of the other great African state. Nigeria now has the largest economy in Africa with a GDP of $510 billion in 2013 compared to South Africa's $370 billion. Its 7 percent annual GDP growth rate during

---

[32]The data on South Africa are drawn from these sources: World Bank (2014); *The Economist* (2014a); U.S. Central Intelligence Agency (2014).

the last decade is also higher than South Africa's. Of course, this is due in considerable part to Nigeria's rich oil and gas industry, which accounts for roughly 14 percent of GDP and is attracting much foreign investment. One must immediately stress the fact that its large population of 170 million (one in five people in sub-Saharan Africa are Nigerian) is expanding rapidly: the United Nations predicts a rise to 440 million by 2050. As a result, the high unemployment rate of 24 percent in 2011 may well get worse. Further, the number of those living in poverty has actually increased reaching a whopping 70 percent. Inequality is also high at 0.44 on the gini index. Despite its lucrative energy resources, GDP per capita remains low—at $2,700, it is about half that of South Africa. Most Nigerians live on less than $2 per day. Nigeria also suffers from lack of physical infrastructure, including bad roads mired in traffic jams and frequent power shortages. Natural resources do not guarantee development and prosperity, as noted, unless the state is strong enough to put these to good use.

Unfortunately, the Nigerian state's capacities are far less developed than South Africa's. There is a measure of path dependency here: Nigeria was ruled indirectly whereas South Africa had large settler populations—the former leaving little mark, the latter a thicker institutional imprint. Accordingly, Nigeria has trouble passing legislative reforms, and it lacks an efficient property registration system—whilst its judicial system is notably slow. Further, the state never had the capacity, in part because of democratic pressures, to repress wages so as to use the surplus for developmental purposes. Then the funds derived from oil were either taken by the elite or spent on immediate gratification, particularly at election times—as these elections were "managed" rather than the real expression of popular control. The Nigerian case is tragic precisely because oil monies were so to speak free-floating, making the creation of a stronger state able to force development at least possible to imagine. Corruption is rampant and debilitating. The head of the central bank reported in 2013 that $20 billion in oil revenues had gone missing; he was fired within days. Tax collection is extremely ineffective, thereby limiting the state's ability to maintain order and protect its citizens. Abductions and kidnappings are so high that they are a routine part of everyday life. In 2013, Nigeria had the most kidnap attempts of any country in the world, accounting for 26 percent of all such recorded incidents. Mexico was second with 10 percent and Pakistan was third with 7 percent. Kidnapping is a lucrative business as most companies and other organizations cough up the money because the state is seen as helpless in dealing with the issue.

Regional variation lay behind the vicious war occasioned by Biafra's attempt to secede. Though that conflict is in the past, ethnic and religious tensions are increasing between the North and the South. In particular, the state has been ineffective in dealing with the Islamist extremists, Boko Haram, in the north-east part of the country since 2009. The most recent example is the kidnapping of over 200 school girls, which has attracted much international attention but very little effort by the government to address it. The conflict with Boko Haram is estimated to have caused over 4,000 deaths, many as a result of the collateral damage caused by the errant counter-attacks of the Nigerian army. In fact, Nigerian soldiers have notoriety for being as bad as terrorists and insurgents in terms of plundering, extortion, and violence. The United Nations estimates that nearly 400,000 people have been displaced recently as a result of the conflict.[33]

The comparison between these two African countries is instructive. Both are experiencing economic development. But South Africa has been more successful in maintaining order and overcoming ethnic divisions than Nigeria, bereft of key institutional capacities and unable to stop Islamist extremists operating with impunity. The level of state and nation building seems, as we would expect, to best explain the difference and to predict what may come next.

Indonesia and Turkey can be taken as a pair for three reasons. First, both states were subjected to massive social engineering. The script was changed and a large dose of Westernization (secularism, rights for women) imposed in Turkey, whilst a new national language was imposed and—remarkably—accepted. Second, the armed forces have played a central role as modernizers in both societies, feeling bound to impose military rule if need be to move society forward. Third, both have Muslim populations, albeit the character of Islam in South East Asia has been very different from that in the classical heartland, though contemporary means of communication are now importing a measure of puritanism into the former.

Suharto came to power in 1967 on the back of vicious repression of communism, thereafter presiding over a notoriously corrupt military dictatorship for more than 30 years. Although the army is no longer in power, not least given the opprobrium it drew when resisting the secession of East Timor, its presence is still felt: Susilo Bambang Yudhoyono, president between 2004 and 2014, was a retired general. Conflict in Indonesia has often revolved around religious nationalism. But progress has been made: Aceh separatism was contained in a settlement in 2005 that allowed for the introduction of Sharia law. The historic peculiarity of Indonesia, that of holding such a diverse territory together, may be further cemented by a turn to more inclusive politics.

Certainly Indonesia has recently made remarkable progress economically, growing at about 6 percent annually during the last decade due in part to fiscally conservative policies and limited debt. Its GDP per capita has more than doubled and its poverty rate has dropped from 24 percent to 12 percent between 1999 and 2012. However, while living standards are rising across the board, inequality is growing. During the first decade of the twenty-first century, Indonesia's gini coefficient rose from 0.29 to 0.37. Much of the economy's growth stems from the export of minerals, fish, and palm oil, particularly to China, which means that the Indonesian economy is particularly vulnerable to swings in Chinese demand. The same is true in terms of its banking and monetary system, which is especially exposed to American investment and dramatic swings in the value of its currency.[34]

Progress is as striking in Turkey. Stability here too has increased as the result of a turn to more inclusive politics toward the Kurds—wholly welcome as more than 30,000

---

[33]The data on Nigeria are drawn from these sources: *The Economist* (2013e, 2014b); Kohli (2004) part four; U.S. Central Intelligence Agency (2014).
[34]The data on Indonesia are drawn from this source: U.S. Central Intelligence Agency (2014).

lives were lost in the struggle with the Kurdish Workers Party. Restrictions on Kurdish language and culture have been eased gradually, initially in part to boost Turkey's chances of entering the EU. Nevertheless, tensions and occasional violence remain, so the nationalist question is not finally settled. Indeed, one now has to say that the struggle over national identity has a new front. The secularist establishment is beginning to feel itself threatened by the increasing religious pressures imposed by Prime Minister Erdoğan, keen to cement his influence by becoming President. Just as important is the arrogance that power has brought: demonstrations about a park in central Istanbul led to a more general politicization as the result of violent repression, not least most recently of both the media and the judiciary. There is massive evidence of the new elite's involvement in corrupt property deals.

Still, there can be no doubt but about the economic progress of Turkey. The country suffered considerable inflation and economic volatility in the 1990s, but the Erdoğan government's policies helped stabilize the situation and facilitate development. It now exports a variety of agricultural products as well as consumer electronics, textiles, and clothing and is a leading shipbuilder. As such, Turkey's annual economic growth has been impressive—6 percent during the early twenty-first century until 2008 and 9 percent in 2010 and 2011. However, concerns are mounting that this performance has been driven largely by debt-fueled private consumption and property investment thanks in part to too much "hot money" from the United States and artificially low interest rates in Turkey. In particular, the government has awarded hefty contracts to Turkish construction firms for massive infrastructure projects like airports rather than facilitating investment in industry. Making matters worse, the value of the Turkish lira has been under pressure in the last few years, thanks to Turkey's considerable current account deficit, and the unemployment rate is over 9 percent.[35]

Indonesia and Turkey experienced massive social engineering, and both have developed with considerable pain but with the prospect of great progress, now that harsh military rule has been contained. The retreat of the military allows one to hope for Burma and makes one fear for Egypt. But we leave these cases to one side so as to offer the first of our general comments on the role of Islam in the contemporary world. While it is almost certainly wrong to think of any sort of generalized "clash of civilizations", to use Samuel Huntington's phrase, sources of real tension can be detected. It is vitally important not to "essentialize" Islam, imagining it to be one and one thing only. To begin with, the strength of Muslim sentiments is very much related to the way in which states treat their peoples. Further, it is not the case that Islam is somehow inherently opposed both to democracy and to nationalism. The latter consideration is especially important. A shared national identity, characteristically based on a distinct national language, has the capacity to so integrate people as to undermine any powerful international form of Muslim sentiment. One needs, in other words, to be very careful about speaking of "international terrorism" emanating from the Islamic world, given that most of these

---

[35]The data on Turkey are drawn from these sources: *The Economist* (2014c); U.S. Central Intelligence Agency (2014).

and other terrorists have local aims. But there are some such groups, and they do challenge the established order—often provoking it to actions that lack wisdom, at times indeed exacerbating tensions. These groups characteristically come from the classical heartland of Islam in which Arabic dominates, thereby ruling out national languages on the basis of which independent state formation can take place. All of this can be usefully encapsulated by saying that Islamism can be contained by nationalism.[36] The fact that such national deepening is far from being achieved, on top of which is imposed the militarization of these countries that has already been noted, explains why the Middle East is the fount of much of the danger in contemporary world politics.

Consider finally two Latin American countries—Chile and Mexico—that have been dramatically affected albeit in different ways by the United States. Chilean democracy had a long and successful history before succumbing to the bloody military coup in 1973 that replaced a socialist government with the right-wing regime of General Augusto Pinochet. Not only did the United States back the coup but it also provided advisors to help guide neoliberal economic reform thereafter. Pinochet privatized many services, including education, health care, pensions, and the provision of water and electricity. He also dismantled trade union rights and collective agreements and trampled human rights in horrific ways. The political system was rigged in order to make it extremely difficult for any opposition to control parliament. However, Pinochet was eventually persuaded to stand for re-election: he lost in 1990. Both center-left and center-right have been in power since, both taking care to keep the military out of politics.

There is considerable debate about whether Pinochet's policies, subsequent reforms, or other factors were responsible for Chile's impressive economic development. Whatever the case, Chile generally now follows countercyclical fiscal policy, accumulating surpluses in sovereign wealth funds during periods of growth and high prices for copper, their principal export, and allowing deficit spending during periods of contraction and declining copper prices. From 2003 to 2013, economic growth averaged 5 percent per year, with the export of goods and services accounting for roughly a third of GDP. Financial institutions are strong. Inflation is low at less than 2 percent and unemployment is around 6 percent. Not surprisingly, the country now has the strongest sovereign bond rating in South America. Chile has taken great strides to reduce its poverty rate, which is now about 15 percent of the population. Nevertheless, inequality remains very high with a 0.52 gini coefficient due in part to terribly unequal access to education. The inequality issue has become a political hot potato insofar as it has sparked a vocal student movement (and more recently regional and environmental movements), arguing that rising inequality is the consequence of the privatization strategy. These movements helped re-elect Michelle Bachelet as president in 2014; her government has promised to reduce inequality by reforming the educational, tax, public pension, and electoral systems.[37]

---

[36]Mabry (2015).
[37]The data on Chile are drawn from this source: U.S. Central Intelligence Agency (2014).

Mexico stands in sharp contrast. The party of the Mexican revolution (1910–1920) the Institutional Revolutionary Party (PRI), has had a hegemonic position in Mexico, interrupted only by Vicente Fox's National Action Party (PAN) between 2000 and 2012. Prolonged single party rule creates patronage and cronyism, so the Mexican state has succumbed to a fair amount of corruption. Added to this has been the rise of powerful drug cartels that have engaged in bloody feuding leading to the deaths of tens of thousands. In 2013, Mexican army, navy, and federal police forces took over the country's second largest port, Lazaro Cardenas, on suspicion that it had been infiltrated by drug mafias, whilst Apatzingan, a city of about 100,000, turned into a virtual battleground between drug smuggling gangs and the local population and vigilantes. Police and military ineptitude is so widespread and well known that according to the national statistics institute (INEGI) most crimes, including murder, kidnapping, and extortion, are never even reported to the authorities.

Until the 1970s, the Mexican state pursued a developmental strategy based on tariff protection and financial support for fledgling industries, state intervention in the economy (especially in the oil and electricity industries), and low levels of taxation. Beginning in the 1970s, however, this changed and Mexico opted for neoliberalism and a free trade strategy, thanks in part to the influence of US economic advisors, Mexican economists trained at US universities, and, of course, Mexico's membership in the North American Free Trade Agreement and other trade agreements. Despite a serious debt crisis in the early 1980s and a massive run on the peso in 1994–1995, both leading to two internationally financed bailouts, the Mexican economy has developed with annual growth rates ranging between 2 percent to 5 percent most years over the last two decades. The economy has become increasingly oriented toward manufacturing since NAFTA went into effect and Mexico has become the second largest trading partner of the United States posting $507 billion in two-way merchandise trade in 2013. Unemployment is about 5 percent at present, although this figure must be tempered insofar as some observers estimate that as much as half of all economic activity is in the informal economy, with a good deal depending on remittances from family members working in the United States. That said, over half the population is below the poverty line and inequality is high with a gini coefficient of 0.48 in 2008.[38]

A second general comment concerns the nature of nationalism in Latin America. The break with Spain in the early nineteenth century was made possible because the metropole was engaged in fighting Napoleon, but it was very much an elite affair—not least given the sight of rebellions of the native population, led respectively by Tupac Amaru in Peru and Toussaint L'Ouverture in Haiti. Nationalism did not involve all the people. This is beginning to change, especially in the Andean countries. The national question is far from finished as it is only now, in the early twenty-first century, that the people are entering onto the political stage.

---

[38]The data on Mexico are drawn from these sources: Babb (2001); U.S. Central Intelligence Agency (2014).

Conclusion

We began the last chapter by noting that development is taking place and can now conclude by emphasizing that this takes places through different mechanisms and at varied tempos. The countries of the North will have to reorient their economies to compensate for industries and jobs lost through outsourcing to countries in the South with lower labor costs. Politically, this will be costly in the short run; dislocation is never easy. These effects may be most pronounced in Europe. It may well be that the smaller countries are best positioned to make these adjustments insofar as they have been engaged with the international economy for a long time already and as a result have learned to be flexible. Larger Northern states may have more difficulty. The larger European states are most likely to lose out in another way: if commanding positions are to be taken by the rising powers and newly industrializing countries in international institutions, it is likely to be at the expense of Europe rather than the United States. We turn to these issues and justify our view in the next two chapters.

CHAPTER 5
THE NORTH

The most striking feature about the North in the postwar period has been the increasing integration that has taken place within it. Genuine interdependence has come about under the American umbrella, allowing states in both Southeast Asia and Europe to become formidable players in the world economy. One claim that has frequently been made is that there will accordingly be convergence within capitalist society, with every country moving to a similar set of institutions. We reject this view in the first section of this chapter: capitalist society has been diverse in the past, and there are strong reasons to suggest that it will remain so. We then consider a second claim, curiously different in character from that of the first in that it suggests that a leading edge within capitalist society may challenge the United States. This was once believed about Japan! The demise of that illusion means that we concentrate on the claim that the EU—now larger than the United States both in terms of population and GDP—will become so united as to be able to challenge the hegemonic position of the United States. Our argument in the second and third sections of this chapter will be straightforward and equally negative: the EU is an economic giant but a military worm, wholly incapable of challenging the United States.

Steering mechanisms

Let us recall two background factors. First, the brutal and bloody era of the world wars involving ethnic cleansing, population transfers, and mass murder largely "solved" the nationality question, thereby making it easier to establish domestic order. Second, the postwar settlement brought more security to the region than it had enjoyed previously. Cold war tensions replaced interstate wars. This was the world of "embedded liberalism"—that is, a social world based on respect for markets when embedded in a system of institutions designed to avoid the sort of economic calamity that had contributed to war.[1] We begin this section by pointing to variety within this general category, before insisting that this variety is still present despite the most recent challenges that capitalism has imposed on states—and then explaining why this is so.

A first way for a state to swim within modern capitalism is by means of liberalism. The "liberal" state maintains an arms-length relationship with the economy, grants

---

[1]Ruggie (1982).

extensive freedom to markets, pursues relatively vigorous anti-trust policy to ensure market competition, relies heavily on broad macroeconomic and monetary policies to smooth out business cycles, and tries not to interfere in the activities of individual firms. The United States is often cited as the best example of the liberal model but the United Kingdom, Australia, Canada, and New Zealand are best understood within the same category.[2] Despite much neoliberal rhetoric, these countries do not somehow exemplify laissez faire policies in any complete sense. An enormous part of the American economy depends on military spending, a significant portion of which goes either directly or indirectly to research and development and to technology innovation; still more depends on various welfare state expenditures, particularly for health care and social security for the elderly.[3] The point is not that liberal states are somehow less involved in the economy or less interventionist than other types of states. Rather, the form of that involvement is qualitatively different from that of other types.

This difference is obvious in comparison to a different "statist" form. In this political economy, the state exercises direct influence over individual industries and firms by providing finance, credit, tariff protection, and infrastructural support. Occasionally the government owns, or at least has an ownership stake in, firms in key infrastructural industries, such as railways, telecommunications, and energy, although since the 1980s statist countries have privatized many firms. Japan exemplifies this world but so too does France, the political contours of whose political economy can be usefully noted. The memory of the fall of France in 1940 made postwar politicians and academics determined to reconstruct and to modernize, not least by means of establishing national champions such as nuclear energy, so as to regain a prominent position in the world. Much of this activity was guided by the "indicative planning" of the Commissariat Général du Plan; this allowed leaders from industry, the ministries, and other organizations to convene periodically to exchange information on their plans for growth in an effort to informally coordinate economic activity. The Treasury provided tax credits and subsidies to facilitate the five-year plans that resulted from these meetings. French statism reached its zenith under François Mitterand's regime when the state nationalized a number of firms and banks in the early 1980s. The attempt to have democratic socialism within capitalism lasted for an instant before Mitterand was forced to dramatically reverse course.[4] Statist instincts remain, of course, but uncertainty has marked the means by which they can be applied in the ensuing years.

Corporatist arrangements are typically found in the Scandinavian countries, Germany, Austria, Switzerland, and the Low Countries.[5] The states in these countries promote bargaining and negotiation among well-organized social partners, notably

---

[2]Hall and Soskice (2001).
[3]Block (2008); Campbell et al. (1991); Weiss (2014).
[4]Hall (1986).
[5]Katzenstein (1985).

centralized business associations and labor unions, in order to push economic and social policies that benefit all groups in the society. Postwar legislation in Germany ensured that at the level of the firm, labor would be represented on corporate boards of directors and works councils that would facilitate bargaining between managers and workers over such issues as investment, plant closings, shop floor relations, and the introduction of new production technologies. At the industry level, the state also organized bargaining between employer associations and unions over wages, benefits, and in some cases prices.[6] These issues were more centralized in Scandinavia. National peak associations representing labor and employers struck wage agreements that set the parameters under which industry level deals were subsequently negotiated. In Denmark, for example, the Ministry of Finance plays a key role in these negotiations both as a facilitator of dialogue between employers and unions, and as a participant insofar as the state is the employer of a sizeable proportion of the labor force.[7]

These regimes provide welfare services in different ways. The statist policies of France (but not of Japan!) are extremely generous. In contrast, liberal regimes offer comparatively meager benefits, believing that much should be left to the market. Some programs are means-tested while others, such as social security and health care for seniors, are funded by the contributions of workers and their employers. Contributory programs often involve a mix of public and private sources. In the United States, for instance, senior citizens are eligible for benefits under the state's social security program but they may also supplement those benefits from the proceeds of their private individual retirement accounts; similarly, national health insurance for seniors is often supplemented with the purchase of additional private insurance. The variety that we stress expands when corporatist welfare policies are examined.[8] Christian democratic welfare states like Germany's provide more generous status-based programs that are connected to an individual's employment. Metal workers receive certain health insurance and retirement benefits based on their employment, with different benefits going to schoolteachers and construction workers—differences being based on negotiated agreements in each economic sector. Further, Christian democracies rely on the family to provide some support; this is why in Southern European countries, the benefits for the young and the elderly are less generous than those for working adults. In contrast, Scandinavian social democratic welfare states offer the most generous benefits, universally available and funded largely if not entirely by the central government.

At the base of this variety lie different tax systems. Liberal states, given their laissez faire ideology, favor low levels of taxation based heavily on income and social security taxes. Statist France and corporatist Germany tend to impose somewhat heavier tax burdens, while social democratic corporatist states levy the heaviest burdens of all. In

---

[6]Streeck (1997).
[7]Esping-Andersen (1985); Pedersen (2006, 2011).
[8]Esping-Andersen (1990, 1996).

light of the fact that social democratic states are bolstered by strong labor movements, it might be surprising that their tax regimes rely heavily on regressive taxes, notably steep value added or national sales taxes on goods and services. But this is a revenue source that is more insulated than are income taxes from business cycles and other fluctuations in the economy. Such stability helps maintain generous welfare through thick and thin.[9]

In sum, states can be arms-length regulators, strong economic players, or facilitators of bargained agreements. But states are always connected to their economies. During the early days of capitalist industrialization in Europe, the state played an important albeit rudimentary role in defining property rights, regulating business, and providing minimal protection for workers; the state was equally pivotal in providing corporate charters, infrastructure, subsidies, and property rights for the economy in the United States.[10] What is most noticeable in the more recent historical record are the comparative institutional advantages of different regimes. Liberal political economies enable firms to compete by making decisions quickly, keeping costs low, and moving capital rapidly from sector to sector and from region to region. Statist and corporatist regimes try to enable firms to compete by producing high quality products and by ensuring a high degree of cooperation between labor and management, creating a well-educated labor force, ensuring wage and price stability through bargaining and through offering generous welfare supports to facilitate the sort of economic restructuring that enables business to be competitive internationally.[11] This is not to imply, however, that all European states are doing equally well. Those in the southern region, notably Spain, Italy, Greece, and Portugal, are not. Their fates, of course, have been tied especially tightly to the 2008 financial crisis.

Since the mid-1970s, states have come under pressure to change their economic and welfare policies. Capital has gained the ability to move from one country to another faster and in greater volume, thanks in part to the breakdown of the Bretton Woods system and the subsequent scrapping of capital controls. Some welcome this: neoliberalism has at its core a deep belief in the benefits of free markets. Others are concerned that the ability of firms to rapidly shift investments from one country to another will undermine the various regimes we have identified. These critics warn that states will increasingly need to compete against each other to retain and attract capital investment. To do so, it is argued, they will have to realign their institutional arrangements with the liberal model. In other words, they will have to grant firms more autonomy to do as they please without having to worry about the interests of government, labor, or other actors. States will have to "race to the bottom" by reducing taxes, welfare spending, and the regulatory burden on business. If they fail to do so, capital flight will result, and this will precipitate plant closings, job loss, unemployment, and poor economic growth. Ultimately, according to this view, state sovereignty is at risk: the only way to control capital will be for

---

[9]Campbell 2005; Kato (2003).
[10]Polanyi (1944); Roy (1997).
[11]Hall and Soskice (2001).

nation-states to relinquish their powers to regulate economic activity to international organizations, such as the WTO and the EU.[12]

Neoliberalism certainly gained enormous traction in Anglo-Saxon countries, most notably Britain and the United States but also in Canada and Australia. Tax cuts, especially for the wealthy, reductions in government spending on social programs, a reduction in the political regulation of the economy, and a shift from demand-side Keynesian-style macroeconomic management to supply-side monetary policy have all been in evidence. Nonetheless, there is little indication throughout the North as a whole of institutional convergence on the liberal model of low taxes and government spending nor that serious economic problems result for countries that fail to pursue that approach.[13] Germany, for instance, has tempered neoliberal rhetoric, thanks to its long ordoliberal tradition, which favors not just the market but also the provision of adequate protections for the population. The same is true of the Scandinavian countries with their strong ideological commitment to social democracy. Post-tax/post-transfer income inequality has remained significantly lower and more stable in these countries during the late twentieth century with gini coefficients hovering around 0.24 than in most continental European countries and especially the Anglo-Saxon ones.[14] Some corporatist institutions were modified in Sweden and Denmark, but they were most certainly not decimated. In Denmark, for example, corporatist wage bargaining was decentralized; national wage bargaining persists there but now only as a loose framework within which harder bargaining transpires at the industry and then the firm levels later on.[15] France too pulled back from indicative planning and abolished the Commissariat Général du Plan, but the state still engages in industrial policy, oversees the national educational and training system, and mandates that social benefits agreed to as the result of corporatist-style bargaining apply even to employees not belonging to the unions. Though the political efforts to roll back business regulation, welfare spending, and taxes have been general, there has been little sign that this has been successful everywhere. So, there is no truth to the view that the end of the nation-state is nigh.[16] Five factors can be distinguished explaining why this is so.

To begin with, states are not helpless in the face of increased global economic pressures. After all, states are partly responsible for the rise in international trade and capital mobility in the first place because they have deliberately lowered barriers to trade and investment. As such, they can surely reverse these trends if they want—as occurred during the interwar years albeit with disastrous consequences. States can also block

---

[12]A second, rather different pressure for change must be mentioned. Were global interactions to be somehow curtailed, northern states would still face huge pressures from demographic change. Populations are getting older and birth rates have been declining. More people are depending on social security, health care, and other welfare benefits while the number of people working and paying taxes to support these programs is shrinking. This demographic squeeze will put increasing fiscal pressure on states.

[13]Campbell (2004), chap. 5; 2005; Swank (2002).

[14]Kenworthy (2004), pp. 128–130; Mann and Riley (2007).

[15]Campbell and Pedersen (2014).

[16]Guéhenno (1993).

these sorts of reforms if political forces are strong enough to resist change. This is why the Scandinavian countries have not abandoned the highest taxes and most generous welfare state programs in the world. Further, even when states make concessions in one area, such as by lowering corporate profit taxes, they can compensate in other areas, such as by devising new taxes on Internet commerce or cross-national financial transactions.[17]

Second, when states try to mimic the institutional practices of their counterparts elsewhere, they typically translate them into local contexts in ways that do not fully supplant current practices. When the Japanese state privatized the national telephone company in 1984, it also developed a powerful regulatory ministry to supervise many aspects of the new private firm's operations, including pricing and technology development. These state capacities were much more in line with Japan's traditional statist model than the alternative liberal model. Put differently, in the face of globalization, states have reregulated rather than deregulated their economies. States have not withdrawn from the economy but rather reoriented themselves to it.[18]

Third, firms do not compete only on the basis of costs. Even if they can find cheaper labor or lower taxes somewhere else, they do not automatically move their operations there if they recognize that they enjoy other competitive advantages where they are currently doing business. Firms operating in the Scandinavian countries may face much higher taxes and labor costs than their competitors elsewhere, but they enjoy such off-setting advantages as a well-educated work force, peaceful labor-management relations, excellent infrastructural support, and a clean environment. Capital may have become increasingly mobile internationally, but firms recognize that they can compete on the basis of comparative institutional advantage as well as comparative cost advantage. States are a crucial source of comparative institutional advantage: minimum wages, maternal and paternal leave protection, and guaranteed paid leave to care for sick children and aging parents can improve worker productivity and thus firm competitiveness.[19] Firms recognize this and so oppose attempts to undermine these institutional advantages. Although German firms pay relatively high wages and benefits to their workers as a result of the corporatist bargaining described earlier, they resisted calls in the 1990s to dismantle these arrangements precisely because they understood the advantages that accrued from them, such as very cooperative labor-management relations that facilitate high quality production and the ability to be flexible in the face of the rapidly changing market demands that are associated with globalization. These are things that the state has facilitated and that have bolstered Germany's international competitiveness for decades. Many firms want to preserve this.[20]

---

[17]Campbell (2003).
[18]Vogel (1996).
[19]Heymann and Earle (2010).
[20]Thelen and Kume (1999). Nevertheless, during the 2000s in at least some sectors of the German economy some parts of the corporatist model began to erode. Whether this signified the emergence of a dual labor market or a more widespread shift toward an entirely new and more neoliberal model of capitalism is a subject of much debate (e.g., Palier and Thelen 2012; Streeck 2009).

Fourth, states can utilize existing institutions to adapt to their changing environments. The corporatist institutions of Denmark and Finland have traditionally helped protect existing investments in the economy, only slowly and incrementally allowing for the adoption of new technologies and the manufacture of new products. But with the advent of globalization, this sort of conservative corporatism was transformed into more a competitive and creative form that helped target new twenty-first-century enterprises, occupations and industries for growth and development in ways that enhanced national economic competitiveness. The state transformed the purposes to which its existing institutions were being put without transforming the institutions themselves.[21] There were adjustments but adjustments in keeping with the state's own institutional legacy rather than some neoliberal blueprint.

Finally, states may make fairly radical institutional adjustments in the face of globalization but without necessarily kowtowing to neoliberalism. Consider the way in which Ireland changed in the 1980s so as to escape from its prior lackluster performance. The state organized a number of social partnerships at the local and regional levels involving business, labor, and other stakeholders. The idea was to facilitate corporatist bargaining in order to stimulate the development of new cutting-edge firms and industries in things like information technologies and pharmaceuticals. To be sure, this move was coupled with neoliberal tax reforms affording corporations especially low tax rates. Thus, the Irish state blended elements of corporatism and neoliberalism into a mixed model that led to the highly successful Celtic Tiger of the 1990s. When it shifted even more in the neoliberal direction, things fell to pieces in part due to the collapse of a housing bubble that the tax cuts helped spawn, which is why change is afoot again.[22] The important lesson here is that states can cope with globalization by shifting either toward or away from neoliberalism—shifts that are driven as much by politics as they are by any sort of economic imperative associated with globalization. There is no guarantee that neoliberalism will work, in which case the state might very well try something else.

So states do not necessarily change in the face of globalization, and if they do change, they do not necessarily adopt a neoliberal approach—and if they do adopt such an approach, they may abandon it if it does not work out as planned. None of this is to say that globalization is the only force precipitating changes in states. Politics matters too. For instance, shifts in nationalist ideologies about ethnic differences can cause dramatic change. The pillarization of politics and the consociational bargaining associated with it gave way recently in the Netherlands to majoritarian democracy as these religious differences became less salient politically.[23] Of course, the loss of difference in that regard is offset by the emergence of contentious politics concerning immigration. These issues are especially salient within the EU, to which we can and should now turn. For, if there is an area of the world in which nation-states are purportedly losing their powers it is

---

[21]Ornston (2012).
[22]Ó Riain (2014).
[23]Jones (2008).

surely here. No greater test of our central contention of variety within capitalism could be imagined than the EU. Is this an organization that will end national diversity?

The European Union

No region in the history of the world has created more insecurity—more wars, more deaths, in its heartland and throughout the world—than has Europe, especially in its dark and vicious twentieth century. The realization that the core of Europe has become a zone of peace and prosperity can only make one weep with joy.[24] It is not surprising in consequence that a slew of commentators suggest that Europe may "run" this century, given that its "vision of the future" has more to offer than "the American Dream."[25] Hold on! An equally familiar set of commentaries are issued from time to time about the failings of Europe, such as the "democratic deficit" seen in the way in which the main elements of the failed constitution were foisted on its peoples.

The oscillation between these extremes rests on a failure to understand the nature of European institutions. European integration has had a long and complex history. Particularly notable has been its curiously stop-go character: just when stalemate seemed in place, a sudden lurch forward occurred. The passing of the Single European Act (1987) and ratification of the Maastricht Treaty (1992) exemplify this pattern. This unpredictability deserves emphasis as it makes one realize that the future of Europe is by no means closed. Who after all would have predicted thirty years ago that the end of communism would allow so many new states to enter the heartland of Europe, most in NATO and the EU, with such astonishing success? But what is Europe now? Will it become, as enthusiasts suggest, a federalist area equivalent to the United States? Arguments over the level of integration within Europe often boil down to interpretations as to whether a glass is half full or half empty. There is no intention here to deny integrative developments, certainly in the economic realm and to a lesser extent in the legal sphere. More than 20 percent of European GDP is traded internally, a figure which amounts to half of all world trade; critically, new members from the East have abandoned their old external markets and are as closely tied to the EU as are earlier members. This is effectively a single market within which the capitalist class moves with ease.[26] Nonetheless, the argument here is of the half empty variety.[27] The justification for this skepticism is simple: there are clear constraints to further integration. The purpose

---

[24]One complexity needs to be borne in mind at all times. The nature of "Europe" was, is and always will be "essentially contested." Russia is part of the same landmass, with some Russians and more Europeans hoping that arrangements can be found to draw it within the core European sphere, thus replicating the marvelous success of European policy in integrating Central European and Baltic states. Of more immediate concern is the fact that some countries in the EU are not part of NATO, while a key member of NATO, Turkey, is not a member of the Union—to the irritation of the United States.

[25]Leonard (2005); Rifkin (2004).

[26]Fligstein (2008).

[27]Moravscik (1998).

of this section is to specify four home truths upon which our skepticism rests; they should be borne in mind by those imagining that transnationalism will increase within the EU.

The first truth is implicit in the account given of the origins of the European project. The rational calculation of states created the EU and its precursors, and those calculations remain in force today. Consider some powerful but banal examples. First, the collapse of communism famously led Margaret Thatcher to get in touch with President Mitterand in order to ask "what should be done with the Germans?" Thatcher's views about Germany reflected prejudice rather than reality, but the analytic point about state calculation should still be retained. For, geopolitical calculation was quite as much at work in France's response to this huge change. If one element was the insistence that Germany be tied to Europe by means of the euro, still more striking was France's return to the NATO command structure—a decision which had at its heart the desire to keep Americans in Europe so as to balance reunified Germany. Secondly, consider the bargaining at the December 2002 Nice summit on enlargement, some details of which were leaked to *The Economist*. This was a forum at which Bismarck would have felt at home: "If you give me this, then I'll give in on that issue" was the characteristic tone of the meeting, especially insofar as voting rights for new states were concerned. Similar points can be made about the new institutional arrangements ratified in 2009: state interests have been protected, with the role of the European Commission falling ever lower in comparison to that of the key intergovernmental institution, the Council of Ministers. Third, skepticism needs to be shown to the claim, far too frequently made, that the Franco-German condominium is losing its salience within Europe: it was these powers that played the decisive role in choosing the first European president. Finally, attention should be given to empirical work probing behind the ideology of integration so as to examine its realities. Francesco Duina took two directives, those on equal pay and on air pollution, and then examined the extent to which different countries actually implemented rules suggested to them. Analysis of three countries per directive produced a picture of very considerable variety. Implementation was likely to succeed when it fitted with previous policy choices and had the support of national pressure groups; when the history and group organization of a nation-state pointed in a direction opposed to the directive, implementation was likely be fudged, delayed, or ignored.[28] States have divergent interests that constrain the possibilities for greater transnational unity within Europe.

Nowhere is this more obvious than in struggles over monetary policy. The euro is not a currency over which there is central, unified control similar to that of the Federal Reserve in the United States—in addition to the fact that ten states in the Union, including the United Kingdom, Sweden, and Denmark, do not belong to that currency at all! The institutional structure of the euro has led to major crisis. The nation-states within the euro zone that are now in deep economic trouble were able to borrow at very low interest rates because of the presence of the German economy within that

---

[28]Duina (1999).

zone, blessed with large surpluses which were invested abroad. The fact that the first country in trouble was Greece led many, especially in Germany, to believe that fiscal irresponsibility was to blame. Had Ireland been the first country to suffer, it would have been clear—given its budget surplus and low debt—that this was not the case: fiscal imbalances and resulting property bubbles mattered much more. The policies to deal with the euro crisis have probably been mistaken: austerity has been imposed instead of sustained policies to resolve bank indebtedness and to increase competitiveness.[29] Here are revealed important national divisions over monetary policy matters. Taxi drivers in Dublin, for instance, curse the Germans for the pain they have inflicted on the Irish economy through their management of European monetary policy. The Germans themselves are torn over whether to let the problem countries manage their own national currencies again, institute a system of dual citizenship with a more vigorous European parliament as the key institution for generating a truly Europe-wide perspective, or promote a deepening of aid from the European north to south in order to deepen European solidarity.[30] In sum, Europe does not have a currency whose institutional architecture is in any way equivalent to that present in the United States. The euro has survived, but it is weak as austerity is ensuring very low growth for the continent as a whole. In the longer run, the structural problem remains unresolved. Germany's surpluses remain too large: their absorption elsewhere led and will continue to lead to bubbles in countries which borrow easy money—with such crises in the end, as some Germans begin to realize, hurting their own country by depriving it of key export markets.

All of this underlines the key point, namely that Europe is certainly not a fully transnational or supranational state. This is not to say that Europe is simply a fragmented constellation of self-interested members. It has succeeded admirably in passing a large number of rules governing its members—some of which are non-binding guidelines passed by unanimous consent and some of which are binding laws passed by majority vote. But particularly in areas that do not involve commerce, the fact that member states have different preferences and that decision-making involves various combinations of representation, deliberation, communication, and negotiation means that it is often difficult to discern a shared strategic European vision. This puts Europe at a distinct disadvantage, particularly in diplomatic matters, when it rubs up against the United States, the rising powers of the BRICs, or sovereign actors whose vision is much more unified, thanks precisely to their having a more sovereignty-oriented perspective. As Michael Smith put it, "while the EU is what some might describe as a 'commercial superpower,' in other areas of its external action it is decidedly stunted."[31]

Secondly, it is crucial to remember that the EU is in a fundamental sense weak, not the Leviathan made much of by most Eurosceptics. The EU is able to fiscally extract only about 1 percent of the GDP of the member states, which is far less than the

---

[29]Legrain (2014).
[30]Hann (2013).
[31]Smith (2013), p. 657.

proportion that the various nation-states take from their societies—characteristically between 35 percent and 45 percent of national product. "The existing budget ceiling," the European enthusiast Loukas Tsoukalis notes, "is simply unrealistic and inconsistent with officially stated objectives."[32] Further, plans to allow for direct taxation have been dropped. It remains the case that the Union by and large has only one policy on which it spends large amounts of money, indeed most of its own budget, namely the Common Agricultural Policy. For similar reasons negotiations with the rising economic powers of the world have lacked real substance.[33]

Remembering this basic fact gives a sense of perspective about the key question of identity, the third area in which skepticism is needed. One of the most firmly established generalizations of comparative historical sociology is that social movements—and the collective identities that inform them—gain force when state demands are placed upon civil society. Perhaps the key social process creating identity has traditionally been that of citizenship struggles over taxation. As the EU makes few fiscal demands on its members, a sense of European identity is unlikely to be created through popular struggles. European identity is at present very limited. All opinion polls show that national identities trump those of Europe in every single country of the Union. There are great differences between countries, with loyalty to the European project characteristically being higher in countries that suffered badly in the war compared to those that did not—between, for example, Holland and Denmark. In any case, identities are not simple, with many having multiple, overlapping and changing identities. But national loyalty remains the most important. Attitudes to Europe are path dependent: they follow the characteristic histories of the nation-states involved.[34]

Crucially, opinion polls also make it quite clear that the EU is essentially an elite affair, with strong support throughout Europe habitually being found in high socio-economic status groups. In this connection, it is worth considering language. The linguistic repertoire that Europeans will need in the future is a two plus or minus one language regime. One necessary language would be English, the world language used most often in EU affairs, with the second being that of one's nation-state. The minus in his formula refers to Great Britain, with the plus being the need to speak a minority language when one's nation-state has a different tongue. It has been claimed that this repertoire will help solve European problems.[35] We are not so sure. Europeans are good at learning languages. But to be really sophisticated, to be able to perform at a high level in other languages is difficult.

Recent work by Neil Fligstein makes one realize still more that European identity is limited.[36] Less than 3 percent of Europeans live outside their own countries, with the number of students spending significant time abroad being scarcely higher. Europe

---

[32]Tsoukalis (2003), p. 136.
[33]Smith (2013), pp. 659, 665–66.
[34]Medrano (2003).
[35]Laitin (1997).
[36]Fligstein (2008), Chapters 5 and 6.

seems to have three core populations: a small number (13 percent) think of themselves as Europeans, an additional number (43 percent) sometimes think of themselves Europeans, while the largest number (44 percent) has no European identity. "Given the right circumstances, 56 percent of people in Europe think of themselves as Europeans (13 percent + 43 percent). But under other social conditions, 87 percent might think of themselves as mostly having a national identity (43 percent + 44 percent)."[37] At a minimum, this suggests that there will be a limit to popular enthusiasm for the Union—as seems apparent from the decline in numbers of those voting at European elections. At a maximum, one might expect something worse. The mood of nationalism is now changing. Nationalism was once an elite project, an element of forced developmental planning designed to help to compete with the leading edge of power. In Europe, it now seems that elites wish to be part of the action within a territorial frame larger than that of a single nation-state, although they doubtless feel that this is the best strategy for their countries. The rise of varied nationalist social movements opposed to further integration suggests that those who are left behind and caged within national borders—that is, groups other than the elites—resent the creation of a world that disadvantages them. The point is that reactionary and nativist nationalism will limit the possibilities for further European integration. Ten of the 20 member states in the 2014 EU parliamentary elections saw large increases of support for the radical right. This was generally considered to be a political earthquake.

The fourth reason why we are skeptical about further increases in unity within Europe involves the issue of Europe's liberal achievements. Economic integration is secure even though the large states breach rules as to budget limits with impunity. Minority rights are equally secure, at least in comparison with the historical record. States wishing to join the Union must change their societies to gain admission, a force entirely for the good. Still, self-satisfaction is most certainly not in order. Geopolitical peace makes possible liberal consociational arrangements of all sorts largely because the "unitariness" of the state is less important when there is no immediate prospect of war. To that extent liberalism has contributed, for example, to the consolidation of multinational Spain. But the brute fact about nationalism remains that ethnic cleansing has taken place within Europe in the last century, most recently of course during the last Balkan wars. So liberalism's capacity to mollify and compromise came into full force only when none of the great problems of the first half of the twentieth century remained. One might further note the intent of Europe to prevent immigration from the South and the East, that is, its desire to remain white and Christian, which has surely played an important role in the EU's reticence in admitting Turkey to the club, though this is now more understandable given Prime Minister Erdoğan's recent authoritarian behavior. Finally, the role played by European states since 9/11 in aiding and abetting the rendition of prisoners suspected of terrorism, at times to centers within Europe at which torture was used, places very serious questions about Europe's

---

[37]Fligstein (2008), p. 4.

supposed liberalism.[38] The emergence of right-wing nationalist parties, already noted, adds depth to the general point. While these parties have operated mostly on the political fringe, they have had some notably prominent success. The Danish People's Party was the lynchpin in a conservative government that ruled for a decade beginning in 2001. This helped push Danish politics to the right in a neoliberal direction and led to the reduction of welfare benefits to residents who were not Danish. More recently, Switzerland voted against the free movement of labor in Europe—a referendum pushed hard by Switzerland's small nationalist party. Switzerland, of course, is not a member of the EU but it has many agreements with the Union, and these are now in jeopardy—as is the very notion of free movement, given that many countries in the EU dislike it too.

It is worth concluding these comments on the institutional character of the Union by repeating what was said at its start. The fact that the limits to integration have been stressed here should not be taken as a claim that integration has no significance. Distinct nation-states may react to directives of the Commission in different ways, but the fact that a single agenda is placed before so many states at the same time may in the longer run diminish variation. Still, the fact remains that the European constitution was rejected—although most of its (weak) proposals came into force anyway, without popular endorsement. In this context, it is useful to remember that successful federalism often depends upon the presence of a *Staatsvolk*.[39] In the absence of a dominating people, federalism can only work when it is combined with consociational arrangements designed to reassure minorities. Given that there are not enough Germans to form a *Staatsvolk* in Europe, stability may well depend upon allowing the blocking powers of small states to remain. With this in mind, we turn to a discussion of the transatlantic community.

The transatlantic community

Europe has been changed as much by external as by internal forces.[40] It will be helpful to recall the classic treatment of political community offered by a team led by Karl Deutsch.[41] Alliances were compared with security communities, both amalgamated and pluralistic. Emphasis was placed on the necessity for a leading power to help construct a security community, habitually in the midst of a shared sense of threat. The maintenance of community depended, however, upon some sense of shared value and a firm commitment to talk and bargain rather than to polarize and fight. Pluralism necessarily meant the presence of greater levels of conflict, but this could be seen as a safety valve: the flexibility of pluralism was to be preferred, in circumstances of difference, to the

---

[38]Anderson (2009), chapter two.
[39]O'Leary (2001).
[40]Katzenstein (2005); Ripsman (2005); Miller (2007).
[41]Deutsch et al. (1957); Adler and Barnett (1998).

brittleness likely to result from amalgamation.[42] The subtlety of this position has been abandoned in recent years, replaced by an oscillation between extremes as violent as that already noted concerning European internal affairs. Powerful voices suggest that the levels of conflict between the United States and Europe are now so great that divorce is in the cards.[43] In contrast, equally powerful voices expect a return to a unified voice for the West.[44] An understanding of the transatlantic relationship will show that this opposition between divorce and absolute love is as false now as it has been since 1945.

There have long been ties between North America and Europe by which the flow of ideas, norms, values, and practices—not to mention trade—have occurred.[45] But during the postwar era, genuine attempts were made to beef up and amalgamate the transatlantic relationship, to create a situation of absolute love in which both sides of the Atlantic would see the world in exactly the same way. This was especially true at the elite level.[46] All those CIA-funded Congresses for Cultural Freedom sought to cement a shared identity. Still, how extensive and deep was transatlantic identity in practice? Identities habitually involve some sort of mix between interest and emotion. If we now revert to continental European cases, the air of calculation rather than of shared identity comes to the fore. As an intellectual, Raymond Aron, despite his fabulous intelligence and carefully nurtured American relationships, was first and foremost French. He is the perfect exemplar of what the community was in practice—a community, for sure, but one that was based on bargaining, calculation, and a combination of shared and dissimilar values. Calculation seems stronger still in Harold Macmillan's celebrated words to Richard Crossman while attached to Eisenhower's headquarters in Algiers in 1942: "[We] are the Greeks in this American empire. You will find the Americans much as the Greeks found the Romans—great big, bustling people, more vigorous than we are and also more idle, with more unspoiled virtues but also more corrupt. We must run [this HQ] as the Greek slaves ran the operations of the Emperor Claudius."[47]

In order to discover the true character of the transatlantic community, there is much to be said for noting the variety of positions that stand between love and divorce. Inequality in gender relations can mean that women are unhappily caged within a relationship, bereft of opportunities for exit, forced to stay but filled with resentments. Complexities lurk here. On the one hand, there are those who would escape if they could, but are prevented from doing so because of the presence of children and the knowledge that divorced men all-too-often refuse to pay for the support of their children. On the other hand stands the psychology dramatized in *Who's Afraid of Virginia Woolf.* The mental state so well portrayed in that play justifies the technical term "co-dependency." This is a world in which resentments are nourished and maintained—a situation of

---

[42]Kagan (2003) Pond (2004); Mowle (2004).

[43]Habermas (2005).

[44]Ash (2004); Ikenberry, (2002).

[45]Rodgers (1998).

[46]Schaeper and Schaeper (1998); Van der Pijl (1984); Berghahn (2001).

[47]Horne (1988), p. 160.

endless complaint bereft of any real determination to change. Divorce is indeed the opposite of absolute love. But matters are far from simple at this end of the scale. There can be trial separations, continued life within the same house, separations that do not lead to divorce—and of course both messy and amicable divorces. On top of all this, one needs to remember that it is not always the case that people occupy one place along the scale in a consistent manner. Resentment is in itself unstable, at once filled with complaint yet stalled in terms of action. And we often wobble back and forth, trying again and again, to give another example, to bargain before finally slipping into resentment. Indeed, human beings suffer from what Marcel Proust termed "the intermittences of the heart." Similar things can be said about the transatlantic community.

Suggestive points about the nature of transatlantic relations rise to the surface immediately. To begin with, countries behave in different ways. The Polish situation has often been close to one of pure love, given the feeling that America helped end the Cold War and assure the freedom of the nation—a feeling of course massively reinforced by links to Polish-Americans. France is complicated. This great republican rival to the United States, now bereft of its empire, has always longed for some way to sustain grandeur—often assuaged by doing much to design the EU but prone, on that very ground, to call for separation from the United States. Second, the affections of states are often as inconstant as those within marriage. France is a classic example. De Gaulle's withdrawal from the NATO command structure stands as a supremely complex move—in the end, a separation without consequence rather than a genuine divorce. German re-unification ended French withdrawal, as noted, for the strengthening of NATO was instantly seen as a way of maintaining the American presence and thereby of limiting the potential of German power. Perhaps this shows the realist calculation of the national interest. But France is not immune from the intermittences of the heart, reacting emotionally to the invasion of Iraq before retreating from a moment of romanticism.

There are also complexities within the United States. Admiration for Germany before World War I was extensive, reflecting massive immigration from Central Europe. World wars changed admiration to distaste. In contrast, the visceral dislike of Great Britain—at the popular level, sustained in part by Irish-Americans and at the elite level, driven by a desire to take over as hegemon—has now been forgotten. Particularly noticeable recently was the ascendancy, perhaps now terminated, of a group of intellectuals, driven by romantic ideals far more than by any traditional sense of national interest. But what matters most is the fact that the United States has an ever present choice within the Atlantic Community. On the one hand stands the demand, articulated by elite and popular forces, that Europe stand up for itself. The continuing presence of American troops in Europe was certainly not planned, and there is much to be said for the view that this presence is historically idiosyncratic—making the occasional call for burden sharing, at times insistent, entirely comprehensible. On the other hand stand the pleasure and benefit of being number one. Power allows one to set the agenda of world politics and thereby to establish a predictable environment. In a nutshell, the United States in this matter is prone to its own intermittence of the heart, that is, to wobble between asking for European independence and not liking for a moment what it sees when such a process seems to be underway.

It is well known that passions can run amok, thereby making rational calculation impossible. But if this is true of the moments of oscillation noted above, quite as important are those moments when sober second thoughts return. Such thoughts arise fundamentally because attention returns to structural constraints that cannot be avoided. In this matter, there is a measure of difference between the United States and Europe, which shed light on the possibilities for a transatlantic divorce—possibilities that in our view are rather slim.

It might be possible for the United States to turn its back on Europe in terms of geopolitics. But this would certainly be unusual historically given the desire of great powers for a predictable political environment. It is unlikely as well insofar as the United States and Europe are each other's most important foreign commercial markets generating nearly $5 trillion in yearly sales. Indeed, no other commercial pathway in the world is as tightly coupled as the transatlantic economy.[48] Further, a multipolar world might well diminish the privileges of seigniorage that the United States enjoys, it being noticeable in this regard that Europe still holds a vast amount of dollars. Europeans face more severe constraints. The most obvious historical constraint has been that of geopolitical fear—that is, awareness of the fact that defense has in the last analysis been guaranteed by the United States with American soldiers being less important as a fighting force than as hostages guaranteeing that the United States would come to Europe's defense if need arose. Geopolitical fears have now diminished greatly, although it is vital to note that the historical experience of Central European countries gives them a continuing appreciation of America's geopolitical role—an appreciation vastly enhanced by Putin's behavior toward Belarus, Georgia, and Ukraine. Just as important is the subjective dimension. The presence of the United States in NATO has been of immense importance to Europeans for the simplest of reasons: the legacy of world war is such that Europeans do not trust each other, and so consider themselves best served by having an external power able to enforce decent rules of behavior. The presence of competing visions within Europe remains a contemporary fact, as was seen both at the time of the last wars of the Balkans and in the rather generalized desire to maintain American troops in Europe so as to limit the power of reunified Germany.[49] These considerations are supported by a further brute fact. A greater measure of European autonomy would necessitate increasing military capacity. There is every reason to believe that any sustained move in this direction would be massively unpopular. By and large, the majority of Europeans—more or less consciously at elite levels, somewhat unconsciously at the level of popular forces—have come to live with an odd, slightly schizophrenic mixture of complaint at American military power in combination with a lack of will to change the situation.

---

[48]Hamilton and Quinlan (2011), p. v.

[49]Divergent national interests can also be seen in the fact that European "governments will not voluntarily give up their over-representation in the G8 or the IMF in favor of a common EU stance" (*The Economist* 2005).

Still even dependent partners may change their minds if they have a significant change of heart. And in Europe there has been a significant shift in feelings from the late 1960s and early 1970s. The benign exercise of American hegemony in the capitalist world did allow for a rather consensual atmosphere within the Atlantic community in the quarter century after the end of World War II. The harsher use of American power led to less consultation, and so to greater European resentment—with neither side really being prepared to change the rules of the game. Many Europeans were deeply opposed to American actions in Vietnam. In a sense, this was the business of the United States alone. This was not true of the consequences of American actions. Lyndon Johnson famously could not decide between guns and butter. Rather than paying for massively increased spending, the United States used its hegemonic powers in a predatory manner by simply printing money. Seigniorage became a serious matter, not least in the extraction of loans from Germany at below market rates.[50] What mattered most of all was that the printing of money to finance the American deficit helped set off the great inflation of the postwar period.[51] More recent events have further compromised Europe's trust in America, notably the shoddy attempt by the Bush administration to form an international coalition to invade Iraq and lately revelations of the US National Security Agency's efforts to spy on European citizens, officials, and even heads of state.

A striking symbol of the change in feeling at an intellectual level was the fact that the thinker most loyal to the United States, perhaps the leading intellect of the postwar community, Raymond Aron, wrote a powerful treatise on the *Imperial Republic*.[52] The great French thinker did not suggest turning away from the United States, but a tone of irritation ran through his elegant treatise. The less sophisticated were more emotional. But what was noticeable in the last analysis was the stability of the oscillation between resentment suggesting action and the reversion to sullen compliance once realization set in that the costs of change were too great. Europeans had learned to whine whilst remaining supine. One remembers the moment when William Perry, President Clinton's last Secretary of Defense, suggested at a NATO meeting that the United States might withdraw its troops from Europe. There was shocked silence followed by an immediate plea to stay. In the end, Europe cringed at the thought of divorce.

Does anybody really think it likely that Europe's status as economic giant and military lightweight will change? A huge shock was administered to Europe by its failure to act cohesively in the face of ethnic cleansing in the Balkans during the last years of the Clinton administration. The promises to produce greater unity at that time have borne no fruit for reasons we alluded to earlier—European states are

---

[50]Treverton (1978).

[51]Smith (1992). U.S. monetary policy was not the only spur to inflation during this period. A sharp rise in energy prices beginning in 1973, notably for oil from the OPEC countries, was terribly important. In the United States annual inflation jumped from 4.2 percent to 9.0 percent between 1972 and 1974, the period of the first oil price shock. And among the 15 EU countries it jumped during the same period from 6.3 percent to 10.1 percent (OECD 2006).

[52]Aron (1979).

not all of like mind in matters of their collective security; reaching compromise if not consensus among them is often fraught with difficulties; and the institutional capacities at hand for security purposes are limited.[53] Despite the appointment of Catherine Ashton as the EU's representative for foreign affairs, who really speaks for Europe in foreign policy matters? The same question can be asked about security issues. The European Rapid Reaction Force has so far been a disappointment, not least perhaps as it is effectively in conflict with NATO's Response Force. Divisions between France and Britain remain great in military matters. Although US military spending has declined since 2010, it is still roughly 50 percent of total military spending world-wide.[54] Europe shows no sign of closing the gap. For instance, all the European members of NATO only contributed about 28 percent of NATO's budget in 2012 while the remaining 72 percent came from the United States—a gap that increased since 2007. Finally, NATO's 2014 defense spending is estimated to be only about 17 percent of world defense expenditures—less than half that of the United States.[55] Beyond that, there is not the remotest sign that Europe imagines its weapons systems working in an autonomous manner. Put differently, the sunk capital of shared technologies really does seem to have created certain lock-in effects where the Europeans are very much dependent on the United States in this regard. Finally, while Britain and France have nuclear weapons, for reasons we explained in a previous chapter the likelihood that they would use them is extremely remote. The point is not that NATO or the EU member states are powerless. After all, they played important roles in Iraq, Afghanistan, Libya, Bosnia, Kosovo, and other conflict zones. The point is that Europe's ability to act decisively in security matters pales in comparison to that of the United States. Furthermore, is it really likely that the euro can triumph over the dollar, when the United States remains the provider of geopolitical security—vitally necessary still in the eyes of the new EU member states of Central Europe? Besides, regardless of the debt holdings we noted earlier, the interpenetration of American and European economies remains very great. Between 2000 and 2010 US firms invested about $1.3 trillion in Europe—over 60 percent of total US foreign direct investment for the decade. 63 percent of world inward foreign direct investment and over 75 percent of world outward foreign direct investment occurred between the United States and Europe.[56] This matters more than trade, since it gives direct access of each other's markets. Europe is economically advanced but it remains fundamentally dependent.

---

[53]Smith (2013), p. 664.

[54]U.S. Department of Defense (2013), p. 7. Although US military spending rose sharply after the terrorist attacks in 2001, it declined sharply from $711 billion to $668 billion in calendar year 2012 and was expected to fall farther in 2013. As of this writing, Congress is arguing about further cuts in 2014.

[55]NATO (2014).

[56]Hamilton and Quinlan (2011), pp. vi–vii.

Conclusion

Let us conclude with a straightforward summary. We argued first that there is great variety within capitalist society and little sign that this is coming to an end. Secondly, it is very unlikely that the EU can challenge the United States, despite its considerable achievements. The internal diversity of the EU makes it impossible for it act together in a concerted manner. This is also true in military matters, with very varied positions being entertained at the time of writing as to how to deal with Putin's annexation of Crimea and challenge to Ukraine. Tensions exist within the transatlantic community, but it remains one in which Europeans, despite complaints, depend upon the United States—and show no sign of taking control of their own destiny. Divorce is hard, inertia more likely.

Nevertheless, the 2014 EU parliamentary elections, as noted, sent shock waves around the world. If the radical right continues to gain traction, it could fracture the European side of the transatlantic alliance. The geopolitical and economic consequences could be severe. One worries that events could so spiral out of control as to cause Britain to exit the EU. The euro itself might crumble. This would surely wreak havoc in international currency markets and cause innumerable headaches for those engaged in international commerce. Concerns about protectionism would seem warranted under these circumstances, which would hobble an already weak European economy still trying to recover from the 2008 financial crisis. One shudders to think what this all might mean for dangerous nationalist tendencies on the continent.

CHAPTER 6
STILL THE STRONGEST POWER ON EARTH?

The functional responsibilities of the state that we have identified are clearly met by the United States. The internal ordering of the state is not in question, although it contains both the splendor of great universities and the misery of prisons and ghettos for too many African-Americans. Just as obvious is the fact that the United States is the only power in the North wholly in charge of its own security, not least as it still benefits from having oceans to protect it from most of its neighbors. That there would be a single type of belonging was of course firmly established in the nineteenth century as the result of vicious civil war, removing the putative national identity of the South. Postwar allegiance to American values has become extremely high, in part because of the flexibility of American national identity: this may be about to change in politics if not society at large.[1] But we have gone beyond these three points to stress the hegemonic powers of the United States. The fact that what goes up comes down gives us the key question for this chapter. Can the position of the United States be maintained?

Great powers certainly rise and fall, as theorists from Edward Gibbon to Paul Kennedy have so often remarked. Three processes seem to be involved.[2] First, a great power can be knocked off its perch, defeated in or exhausted by war—as was true in the twentieth century for Germany and Great Britain when war depleted each state's resource base. A second element can be that of a sideways move of technological innovation. Thorstein Veblen explained the process involved when writing about Imperial Germany and Imperial Japan. Both these states found it possible to adopt the latest technologies without having to take on the institutional baggage of the early leaders.[3] Finally, a great state can decline when it institutionalizes its moment of success, thereby losing its capacity to adapt to changing circumstances. These factors will be taken in turn when looking at the United States, though somewhat messily as they overlap and interweave.

But our insistence on hegemony can also help structure analysis. We saw that hegemonic stability theory claims that a leading power can provide stability to capitalism through the provision of a top currency, defense, and the export of capital for

---

[1]Hall and Lindholm (1999). Wilson (1996) has shown that poor African Americans are strongly committed to traditional American values (i.e., hard work, nuclear family, etc.) but recognize that their capacity to live up to them is often hampered by structural obstacles stemming from their impoverished economic circumstances.
[2]Mann (1988).
[3]Veblen (1915).

development—to which is sometimes added the ability to absorb excess product from the rest of the world due to the size of its domestic market. But a final point drawn from this theory needs to be noted. Decline of hegemony is held, to adapt a famous phrase of Jean-Paul Sartre, to result from the behavior of others. The cost of providing services undermines the leader's own political economy. It is from this condition that calls for burden sharing are derived.

Some initial comments about this theory are necessary. To begin with, the theory is much too neat, not least because American power spread from within a threatened capitalism to much of the globe once its great rival, the Soviet Union, had collapsed. It is just as important to note that the sources of American power have varied over time, particularly insofar as its military capacity vis-à-vis Russia is as strong as ever even though questions have been raised about the health of its economy. Much more important is the need to question the picture of a benign and selfless leader. The United States helped to reconstruct Western Europe and Japan after the war, and it has provided defense for capitalism against its rival. But altruism is a scarce resource, and power can be used to further one's own interests. Recently the United States has, as noted, taken advantage of its possession of the leading edge of power leading some to replace the term hegemony with that of empire. Still, a final point should be added. There is a world of difference between ideological opposition to the United States at the elite level and the increasing impact of the popular culture of the United States. Hollywood is not dead, nor have Converse All Stars lost their cult status.

Given these complexities, it might amuse readers to know a little more about the division between the authors when dealing with American power. One author is a slightly disillusioned European, rather ashamed of its supine position, thereby loath to engage in anti-American feeling because he is all too aware of the continuing strength of that country. The other author is an angry citizen of the United States, so frustrated with the failure of his country to deal with its problems that he is made sensitive to the possibility of decline. Amusement should not mislead: our purpose is empirical, to point to strengths and weaknesses in the position of the United States, well aware that no definitive picture has as yet become apparent. We will describe a glass that is half full and half empty—with readers being asked to decide if the quantities involved vary from 50:50.

Guns and geopolitics

It is as well to start with brute considerations. The United States has undoubted imperial reach. It has 695 military installations in 40 countries and several US territories.[4]

---

[4]U.S. Department of Defense (2013), p. 7. This is a conservative number insofar as an installation is defined by the DOD as being at least 10 acres large and worth at least $10 million. It excludes CIA operations around the world. These numbers are contested and some say they should be much higher. Certainly the number of countries with US military personnel in them is much larger.

This huge predominance is based on the simple fact that it currently spends around 50 percent of total world military budget, outspending perhaps the next seven powers. Of course, this figure misleads in a way: it is very expensive to place an American soldier in the field and very cheap indeed to enroll an Afghan tribesman who can shoot accurately and is further blessed with detailed knowledge of the local terrain. Still, there can be no doubt about the capacity of American weapons to destroy and to do so with minimal human cost, as the use of drones in Afghanistan so clearly demonstrates. Then there is the fact that the United States has the central role in its alliances, most obviously in NATO whose Supreme Commander was, is, and always will be an American citizen. The allies of the United States might well be drawn into American wars; the United States has the privilege of staying out of the wars of its allies.

A crucial point needs to be made about the cost of the military arm. The best way to measure the burden of defense is to consider it as a percentage of GDP. It is true that the United States spends more on defense than any country in the world, but it is very important to stress a basic fact nearly always ignored in public debate. While the sums that the United States has spent and is spending on security are very large, they are currently—even in the midst of engagements in Iraq and Afghanistan, the longest wars in American history—only a small percentage of GDP. Figures are imprecise, for some security spending (military hospitals, the CIA, special funding for ongoing war) does not get counted within this general category.[5] But the figure as a whole has declined from a peak in the mid-1950s of about 14 percent of GDP[6] to a mere 4.4 percent of GDP ($682 billion) in 2012.[7] This suggests that there is likely little merit to the claim of hegemonic stability theory that the great liberal leader is being brought to its knees by bearing too great a share of the burden of defense. Skepticism about that claim is reinforced by further considerations. The danger of excessive defense spending is that it can "crowd out" innovation in other areas by taking the best brains into the military. There is no sign of that in the American case. To the contrary, important industrial innovations, from early manifestations of the Internet and the Global Positioning System (GPS) to breakthroughs in robotics, artificial intelligence, aerospace, hypermedia, and virtual reality were funded by, and in some cases created within, DARPA (Defense Advanced Research Projects Agency), the research branch of the military—hailed by some as the place in which the United States runs an industrial policy.[8] In this regard, one should recall an old tradition in social research stressing the benefits rather than the costs of military spending. There is an element of military Keynesianism in the United States:

---

[5]One should note, on the other hand, that there have been very notable, immediate contributions by the allies to US defense costs. Treverton (1978) gives details of allied contributions to the cost of bases; one should remember that the contributions given by Japan and Europe to the first Gulf War generated a profit for the United States—insofar as one can use language of this sort.
[6]Brooks et al. (2012), p. 18.
[7]Stockholm International Peace Research Institute (2012). China, Russia, and the United Kingdom are the second, third, and fourth largest military spenders at $166 billion, $90.7 billion, and $60.8 billion, respectively.
[8]Block (2008); Weiss (2014).

any deep cuts in defense would probably hurt the American economy. Nonetheless, we must add a pointer to a later consideration of taxes. The actual burden of defense may be light, but in a country that takes a smaller share of total product as taxes than most other states in the North, the fact that the share of defense in 2012 was almost 40 percent of all *discretionary* federal government spending makes it difficult to innovate in other policy areas![9] Nonetheless, military spending per se is not likely to compromise US hegemony for the foreseeable future.[10]

Military might does not fully capture geopolitical power. What matters quite as much is the extent to which one has friends and faces rivals. In both these areas, the United States is well situated. Consider NATO and the South East Asian Treaty Organization (SEATO). We have seen that the former remains vibrant despite tensions within it. There is no sign of it collapsing. The situation in Southeast Asia is more complex, but the legacies of the hatreds born in the 1930s and 1940s remain strong. Hence it is possible to refer to the current move of the United States to reorient its strategies toward the Pacific as an "empire by invitation"—a term originally used about NATO but useful in current circumstances. That move was designed to balance China. A sense of balance is needed here. China's challenge now is infinitely smaller than before: Chairman Mao's crazy threats have been forgotten, with state policy now firmly in the hands of an elite that prides itself on calculation. Militarily, China is of course extremely weak, and news, both official and unofficial, suggests that it still sees internal development as its main task—not least as it has such massive internal problems to handle. Then there is the fact that China depends upon the United States for the open trading system; there is mutual interest as much as rivalry, a situation of co-dependency.

It is also crucial to consider the way in which the United States conducts itself in the world. America has long been involved in a variety of military and diplomatic actions abroad since World War II. Some have been admirable while others have not. Since September 11, 2001, however, things have changed. When the Bush administration announced its intention to invade Iraq, many of America's allies refused to go along. When it was revealed that the evidence justifying the invasion was misleading at best and fabricated at worst, trust in America's leaders was eroded.[11] Moreover, rather than putting an end to Al Qaeda and international terrorism, the adventures in Iraq and Afghanistan, as well as scandals surrounding the torture and abuse of suspected terrorists in Abu Ghraib, seem to have fortified terrorist recruiting and instability in the Middle East.[12] Soon thereafter an intelligence analyst working for the US National Security Agency (NSA), Edward Snowden, leaked thousands of top-secret documents to the press showing

---

[9]Center on Budget and Policy Priorities (2013).
[10]Brooks et al. (2012).
[11]Rich (2006) describes the lengths to which the Bush administration went to massage the evidence to legitimize its invasion of Iraq. All Republican presidents beginning with Ronald Reagan had neoconservative advisors but their grip on foreign policy was strongest under George W. Bush whom they convinced to launch the invasion of Iraq in 2003 to destroy Saddam Hussein's dictatorship (Mann 2013, pp. 278–283).
[12]Mann (2013), p. 301.

that the NSA had been secretly conducting a mass surveillance program for years. Condemnation from the international community was fast, furious, and hypocritical.

So we are in the middle of a period of instability partly occasioned by the aggressive actions of the United States. But the current situation may not last; America has different attitudes it can adopt toward the world. The "unipolar moment" allowed for unconstrained heroism. Policy was influenced by intellectuals such as Paul Wolfowitz, keen to remake the Middle East but utterly naïve in imagining that an occupying army in Iraq would be welcomed with open arms. American involvement there has come to an end, though it is far from sure that the situation left behind looks set to improve on what it replaced. The same is true for Afghanistan now that the United States is pulling out. Iran's position has risen and it seeks nuclear weapons, thereby undermining the key foreign policy goal of limiting nuclear proliferation. Saudi Arabia has been drawn into a regional conflict not unlike the Wars of Religion in sixteenth- and seventeenth-century Europe. But American involvement in Syria was avoided. This has led some to question America's resolve. But this should not be exaggerated. No state doubts the destructive capacity of American military might, and the loss of prestige might well have been infinitely greater had the United States been involved in a war it did not understand and one from which it might well have eventually retreated.

Heroism has characterized American foreign policy before, notably in the involvement in Vietnam. Reflecting on that returns us to a point made earlier. Dire warnings issued about the cost to be borne should Southeast Asia be "lost" proved nonsensical. Many at the time of involvement had suggested that a trading policy would be better, should it be the case that the region became a source of oil production; thereafter, the economic development of the countries in the region has been helped by closer ties to the United States. In a nutshell, the United States did better without this involvement. Thankfully, there was no determining need in the American economy underlying the aggressions of George W. Bush. Trading remains the alternative to heroism. Putting America's own house in order, not least by dealing with the structural imbalances in the world political economy, remains an attractive alternative—and one that is more than ever possible, now that dependence on foreign oil has started to subside.

Dynamism and destruction, dollars, and debts

The great Austrian economist Joseph Schumpeter famously remarked that the secret of capitalism lay in creative destruction, the ability to move from fading industries and technologies so as to embrace new ideas and practices. We will argue that the United States is rather impressive by these standards, by no means as yet surpassed by rivals.

The absolute dominance that the United States enjoyed in the aftermath of World War II, when it created something like 50 percent of world product, has of course gone, as was inevitable once ruined economies recovered. By 1980, market shares at home and abroad for American firms were slipping badly even in industries that they had once dominated.[13] Moreover, after 1976 America began borrowing money from the rest of the world.[14] Germany and Japan benefitted from state-of-the-art technologies and flexible production techniques in automobiles, steel, machine tools, and consumer electronics; further competition came from the Asian Tigers. America was beginning to lose its competitive advantage in the world economy having institutionalized a Fordist production regime based on mass production that was ill-suited for responding quickly to the fickle demands of consumers. As a result, American manufacturers suffered a serious profit squeeze. Between 1963 and 1975, pre-tax profit rates for US firms dropped on average by 46 percent in core industries including rubber and glass products, steel, radio and television equipment, machine tools, motor vehicles, shipbuilding, farm machinery, heavy electrical equipment, railroad equipment, and fabricated metal products.[15]

The recovery of the allies of the United States is of course what it had wanted and so can usefully be seen as much as a sign of strength as of weakness. One should note further that the share of world GDP of the United States came down to about 25 percent in the late 1970s—where it has more or less remained ever since. Crucially, the loss of dominance in manufacturing went hand-in-hand with a shift from manufacturing to services as the backbone of the economy. Between 1947 and 2007, jobs in the service-producing industries increased from 61 percent to 84 percent of the US economy.[16] Not all of the creative destruction involved was economically progressive. Many of the new service sector jobs were in retail, leisure and hospitality, and health care where wages and benefits are not always good. Nonetheless, others were in professional and business services with better compensation packages.[17] In particular, many new service sector jobs were in skill-intensive service industries that increased productivity.[18] Apple was for a short period the largest company in the world in terms of its value on the stock market, and it remains a giant whose products have genuinely changed the way in which the world works. Many of the most striking and innovative companies of recent years in the United States—Microsoft, Facebook, Apple—began in the elite universities of the United States. These universities are without real rivals, and they draw to themselves some of the greatest brain-power in the world. The United States gains the majority of Nobel prizes; many are given to those who have moved from abroad to these intellectual powerhouses.

There are further considerations to be borne in mind, although none are definitive as the indicators are subject to frequent change. The growth rate of the economy is now considerably stronger than that of its rivals in the North, allowing it to deal with

[13]Zucker et al. (1982), p. 14.
[14]This was reflected in deterioration in the current account balance, which in 1976 began slipping into deficit on a more or less permanent basis, reaching $4.9 billion by 1982 and skyrocketing to between $100 billion and $200 billion annually during the 2000s (U.S. Federal Reserve 2013a).
[15]Bluestone and Harrison (1982), p. 148.
[16]Mishel et al. (2012), pp. 327–334.
[17]Mishel et al. (2012), pp. 327–334.
[18]Buera and Kaboski (2009).

debt that much more easily.[19] The current account deficit has declined during the last 5 years and the level of unemployment seems remarkably low to Europeans. Perhaps most striking of all is the fact that American enterprise seems to have recovered its dynamism: the American stock market has recently moved into record territory.

These comments are comparative in nature, and they accordingly suggest systematically revisiting the economic challenge mounted by rising powers. The challenges from Europe and Japan look less serious now than they did a quarter century ago. Our argument about the BRICs has been rather different: even though their share of total world output has dramatically increased, they present no fundamental challenge to the ordering of the world economy. The leading member of the group, China, is still far from dominating international markets, especially in industries based on cutting-edge technologies and well-known brands: eighteen of the twenty top knowledge regions in the world are still in the United States and Europe. American FDI in China in 2009 was more than twenty times larger than China's in the United States.[20] Finally, we have seen that the new generation of rising powers is smaller and starting from a richer—that is, more economically advanced—position than the BRICs during their heyday, making their potential challenge to US economic hegemony considerably smaller.[21]

This is a good moment at which to return to the question of seigniorage. The United States still retains its privileges as the dollar remains the world's reserve currency. This helped the United States manage its recovery from the 2008 financial crisis because by simply printing more money it could spend nearly $1 trillion in Keynesian-style stimulus from Congress, and another $4 trillion from the Federal Reserve's quantitative easing program. Although this contributed to the government's mounting debt, it also reduced the value of the dollar, thereby allowing for an export surge. Further, foreign investors are still willing to buy Treasury Bonds when the world economy gets shaky—which explains the seemingly extraordinary fact that the dollar strengthened in the midst of the 2008 financial crisis.[22] Many countries are not happy, as noted, with the privileged position of the United States. Development still largely depends upon borrowing capital in a currency other than one's own. This is fine in good times, but it can be disastrous under changed circumstances.

Let us turn finally to the level of US debt ($16.6 trillion), very much at the center of debate, not least because of the fear that foreigners might control American society given that fully 46 percent of it is held abroad–with China, the largest foreign owner, holding about $1.3 trillion of US debt, fully 23 percent of all the foreign holdings. We are skeptical about this argument for three reasons. First, the figure of $16.6 trillion is misleading. $4.8 trillion is owed to other American agencies, notably to Social Security pragmatically storing monies for future need. The Federal Reserve Bank holds

---

[19]The OECD forecasts 2.9 percent growth in real GDP in 2014 for the United States in contrast to 1.0 percent for the Eurozone and 1.2 percent for the OECD overall (OECD 2013).
[20]Hamilton and Quinlan (2011), p. vii, viii, xvi.
[21]The Economist (2013a).
[22]Prasad (2014).

$1.7 trillion. Another $4.4 trillion is held within the United States, largely within the private sector. So, only about $5.5 trillion is held by foreign entities, roughly $3.9 trillion of which is in the hands of foreign governments and central banks. Put differently, the United States—able to control its own currency, thanks to the privilege of seigniorage, and possessing an economy valued at between $43 trillion and $164 trillion–owes a paltry $5.5 trillion to foreigners.[23] Second, insofar as China is concerned, it still owns only about 8 percent of America's total outstanding debt. Moreover, China depends heavily on the US market for its exports, and it relies on America for FDI. We have argued that this creates strong economic incentives for China to work with rather than against the United States. Third, wielding foreign debt as a tool for influencing the United States would require several countries to coordinate their efforts. The collective action problems involved would be enormous.[24] Japan holds roughly as much debt as does China. Given the contentious history these countries share, as illustrated most recently in a dispute over rights to the otherwise meaningless Senaku Islands in the East China Sea, it is hard to imagine them cooperating so as to force changes in American policy.

Self-inflicted wounds

Karl Marx once remarked that fundamental social change did not always result from a rising class fighting with and then taking the place of a class in decline. The end of the ancient world saw, in his view, something else: a situation of conflict between classes that was not resolved, resulting in their consignment to common ruin. The real possibility of such ruin in the United States is what concerns us in this section—in which we trace the rise of a radical right, explain that surge, and consider ways in which this may undermine the hegemonic powers of the United States.

The relative consensus of the initial postwar years broke down in the 1960s. The struggle for civil rights for African-Americans, the anti-war movement, feminism, the push for better environmental standards, as well as assassinations marked a tumultuous decade. One result was the alienation of the white male working-class voters, a traditional core constituent of the Democratic Party, resentful of affirmative action programs and taxes for welfare programs that were ostensibly for people different from themselves. The political center of gravity began to shift to the right. The Republican Party closed ranks in an effort to combat stiffer regulations, reduce taxes and limit government spending. The Democratic Party was suffering an identity crisis: organized labor was becoming weaker, while middle-class voters who had fled the Republican Party in response to the scandals of the Nixon administration pulled the party in a

---

[23] Alpert (2013), pp. 227–228.
[24] Similar collective action problems would be involved if somehow the BRICs wanted to flex their collective muscles by dumping their considerable dollar reserves, which amount to a total of $4.6 trillion (*The Economist* 2013a).

more conservative direction.[25] It was the Democrats who passed regressive income tax reform in 1978. But the complete neoliberal assault on taxes, government spending, business regulations, and inflation took place during the two terms of Ronald Reagan. Clinton's administrations continued on the same path, repealing the Glass-Steagall Act, which had separated commercial and investment banking since the 1930s. It also passed legislation prohibiting the federal government from regulating over-the-counter markets for mortgage-backed securities, credit default swaps, and other complex financial derivatives that billionaire investor Warren Buffett called financial weapons of mass destruction. Free markets were believed to work better than those encumbered with government regulation.[26] This diminution of regulation laid the seeds for the financial crisis of 2008.

The explanation for this conservative shift in American politics is complex. Four elements need to be distinguished. First, the collapse of the Soviet Union and the end of the Cold War provided an essential backdrop. Before the collapse, politicians were more accommodating to one another because they believed that excessive divisiveness within their ranks might embolden Moscow in a variety of ways. After the collapse, they were less restrained. Further, conservatives pointed to the end of the Cold War as justification for their belief that markets were good and state interference evil.

Second, money came to have enormous influence. Changes in federal campaign finance laws as well as recent Supreme Court decisions saw the amount of money spent on federal elections soar from $1.6 billion in 1998 to $6.3 billion in 2012, with monies spent on lobbying in Washington jumping from $1.5 billion to $3.3 billion over the same period.[27] Conservatives moved quickly to take advantage of the opportunities involved in new telecommunication technologies. Rush Limbaugh on radio and Glenn Beck and Sean Hannity on television attacked Democrats in Congress and the White House.[28] The provision of funds also explains the rise of conservative think tanks in Washington, notably the Heritage Foundation, the Cato Institute, and the National Center for Policy Analysis, which initiated a war of ideas in Washington exacerbating ideological divisions and partisanship in entirely novel ways.[29] Then, a strategic movement within the legal profession was launched as a counter attack on what was perceived to have been an

---

[25]The declining power of the labor movement was due in large part to the economic restructuring noted earlier. By European standards, the US labor movement has long been weak. The percentage of the labor force that belonged to a union in the 1950s peaked at around 35 percent, among the lowest within the OECD. Historically, union strength lay in the manufacturing sector but as jobs shifted to services unionization rates plummeted. By 1985 only 18 percent of workers belonged to unions and by 2007 it was 13.5 percent. There were other reasons too for this decline including corporate union busting campaigns, federal policies that made union organizing more difficult, and the unions' own failure to organize service sector workers. Outsourcing jobs to foreign countries also contributed to declining unionization rates (Mishel et al. 2012, pp. 327–334).

[26]Campbell (2011).

[27]Center for Responsive Politics (2013).

[28]Eventually the political left responded with its own cable television and radio programing, such as MSNBC's Rachel Meadows and *The Colbert Report* and *The Daily Show* on Comedy Central, thereby further polarizing political life.

[29]Campbell and Pedersen (2014), chap. 2.

increasingly liberal shift toward left-wing precedents being set in the courts in the 1960s and 1970s. This was an effort by conservative forces advocating the development of the "law and economics" approach to judicial decision-making and law school curriculum. The law and economics approach was the legal philosophical equivalent to neoliberalism. Financed by conservative philanthropic foundations and championed intellectually by renowned conservative legal scholars, such as Richard Posner at the University of Chicago, the movement provided free seminars to judges, scholarships to law students, and financial support to law schools around the country, including at Harvard, to teach the law and economics approach.[30]

We have already mentioned the third factor in connection with affirmative action, but it is so central to American life that it deserves systematic treatment. Behind nearly everything that has happened in recent American politics is race, the besetting sin of American life. The unleashing of monies surely derives largely from the continuing racism of American life—seen in the visceral dislike of many white Americans for an African-American President. Importantly, ethnicity is becoming more central to American politics and in ways that resemble the situation in many European countries. The Hispanic community is now larger than that of African-Americans, currently standing at 17 percent of the population and projected to reach 31 percent by 2060. Obama's election to a second term was due in no small measure to overwhelming support among Hispanic and African-American voters. Despite the fact that most Americans—regardless of race and ethnicity—embrace a common set of values about family, hard work, and the like, the country has become extremely polarized in politics, and there is little sign that this will end. Minorities are likely to support social programs and a whole host of other issues—many regarding immigration, such as protecting the borders from illegal immigration, quotas, access of immigrants to education, social welfare, and healthcare benefits, pathways to citizenship, and even voting rights—that look set to dominate domestic politics for years to come.

Finally, an increasingly well-organized movement of conservative Christian religious groups also helped to polarize politics. These groups included the Moral Majority, founded in 1979 by Jerry Falwell, the Southern Baptist preacher and televangelist. The Christian right opposed abortion, homosexuality, same-sex marriage, and Darwin's theory of evolution, and supported politicians who espoused these views. Although they were not particularly interested in economic policy, by pressing Republicans to take more extreme conservative stands on social issues they contributed to the rightward shift and ideological polarization in American politics.

Let us turn to the negative impact that this political polarization is having on the United States, remembering at all times that internal stalemate is starting to have serious repercussions on its hegemonic position within the external world. Money may not be the only thing that makes the world go round, but it is of such importance that we begin there.

---

[30]Teles (2008).

Taxes are the sinews of the state, so we start with fiscal affairs. The United States suffers from persistent government budget deficits and subsequent increase in government debt from about 30 percent to 100 percent of GDP since the 1980s.[31] The situation is likely to deteriorate. Military retrenchment under Obama will help but only a little, as entitlement programs comprise a larger proportion (38 percent) of *total* federal spending. As the baby boom generation grows older and begins to receive Social Security and Medicare benefits, the amount of money required to continue funding these programs will grow significantly, leading to a combined deficit of about 4.5 percent of GDP by about 2030.[32]

Some skeptical comments about the debt problem have already been made. We now add the key consideration: it is not the size of the debt that is of concern but rather the political problems associated with servicing it. The nation's debt would fade quickly if taxes were raised and/or spending was cut. The tax burden as a percentage of GDP in the United States is amongst the lowest in the advanced capitalist world, making the restoration of sound finance eminently possible.[33] But the likelihood of significantly raising taxes seems remote. The insistence on cutting taxes has been enhanced by the rise of the conservative Tea Party movement, many of whose members, ironically, are recipients of both Social Security and Medicare.[34] The likelihood of spending cuts is equally remote. Discretionary spending accounts for only 17 percent of the federal budget so that real change would involve dealing with entitlements of all sorts—that is, tax breaks for the wealthy as well as the costs of public programs.[35] In short, averting the state's mounting fiscal problems would require a significant change in the political landscape—something that does not seem likely. In late 2013, a special congressional committee tried to resolve these budget problems. Some hoped that a Grand Bargain would emerge where politicians agreed to some combination of spending cuts and tax increases. It did not happen. Conservatives blamed liberals for refusing to cut spending. Liberals blamed conservatives for refusing to raise taxes. The reality, however, was that Democrats, who tended to favor higher taxes on wealthy individuals and corporations, admitted off the record that they would not press hard for this because doing so would alienate these groups and thus jeopardize campaign contributions for Democrats in future elections. And Republicans, who tended to favor cutting social programs, also admitted off the record that they would not pursue aggressive cuts in entitlement programs because many of their constituents were retirees who depended on these programs.[36] Not surprisingly, then, the deal finally reached in December did little to

---

[31]U.S. Federal Reserve. (2013b).

[32]U.S. Social Security Administration (2013).

[33]Campbell (2004), chap. 5.

[34]Skocpol and Williamson (2012).

[35]The magnitude of tax breaks should not be overlooked. These constitute a so-called hidden welfare state amounting to billions of dollars of lost revenue annually, thanks to thousands of loop holes in the tax code many of which stemmed from the lobbying of corporations and wealthy individuals (Howard 1997).

[36]Calmes (2013).

resolve the long-term fiscal situation cutting only a paltry $28 billion from the deficit in 2014.[37]

These fiscal problems undermine the competitiveness of the economy. Although the United States spends more per capita on education than the OECD average, the performance of American students (15 year olds) significantly lags the OECD average in mathematics, is slightly below average for science, and is only about average for reading. This does not bode well insofar as the United States has shifted from a manufacturing to a service economy and is competing increasingly in knowledge-based industries like biotechnology, information and technology systems, and software engineering. Part of the problem appears to stem from the fact that educational opportunities are less equally distributed in the United States than they are on average among the other OECD countries. Equally important has been the dramatic decline in infrastructure spending in the United States. Such spending was about $325 billion in 2002 but plummeted to about $225 billion by 2014.[38] If the United States cannot maintain its bridges, highways, telecommunications, and ports, the economy will suffer. This was not lost on the World Economic Forum, which ranks all the countries in the world every year in terms of their overall economic competitiveness. These rankings are based on a number of political and economic criteria. In its 2012–2013 report, the United States' infrastructure ranked fourteenth world-wide, seven positions lower than it was in 2008.[39]

Stalemate in Congress has the capacity to undermine the seigniorage rights that the United States has enjoyed since 1945. The government was shut down for a short period in 2013 over disagreements about the budget, but this was merely a repeat of what had happened in 1994. Rather more serious was the threat made by House Republicans to refuse to raise the government debt ceiling, thereby potentially forcing the government to default on its obligations. This would have led to a downgrading of the country's credit rating and undermined the value of the dollar—the world's reserve currency. Christine Lagarde, head of the IMF, warned that default would result in "massive disruption the world over" and would seriously undermine the world's "trust in the U.S. signature". In the end, the threat was withdrawn. But the lessening of trust seems likely to speed up the move already underway to diminish the central role hitherto played by the American dollar in world affairs. In 2011, China and Japan agreed to direct currency convertibility where their firms would no longer have to use the dollar, with the BRICs announcing a similar agreement. Similarly, the IMF recently added the Australian and Canadian dollars to its list of the world's safest currencies, which already included the euro, the British pound, the Japanese yen, and the Swiss franc. The volatility triggered by economic problems in the United States lies behind the diminution of the dollar's share of global reserves from 71.1 percent in 2000 to 62.1 percent by 2010.[40]

---

[37]Rattner (2013).
[38]*Financial Times* (2013).
[39]World Economic Forum (2012), table 5.
[40]International Monetary Fund (2013).

A final monetary matter involves stepping back a little before moving forward to a divided conclusion, with the split exemplifying the tension between the two authors. The whole world has been subject to financial crisis as the result of American policy. The Asian financial crisis of 1997 was partly caused by adoption of Washington Consensus policies, above all the neoliberal loosening of capital controls that then facilitated the rapid flight of capital out of these countries when foreign investors sensed that economic problems were afoot.[41] Infinitely more serious, of course, was the 2008 financial crisis. There is now widespread recognition at home and abroad that the crisis was rooted to a considerable degree in the deregulation of the financial services industry, famously leading to sub-prime mortgages, which were then securitized and traded around the world. Crucially, this created various housing and asset value bubbles that depended upon the ability to borrow the vast amounts of money that resulted from global financial imbalances. Only intelligent policy makers, acting to save the banking system in a way absolutely opposed to neoliberal theory, were able to avert a second great depression.

Neoliberalism and American leadership were blamed for the crisis, thereby making many elites throughout the world aware that the international monetary system did not rest in a safe pair of hands.[42] That feeling remains. Of course, the Dodd-Frank Act was passed mandating a vast array of new regulations governing the US financial services industry, including federal oversight of mortgage lending practices, the securitization of mortgages, and their trading on over-the-counter markets. But that was not the end of the story. Even at the height of the crisis, neoliberals in Congress pushed back against the size of the bailout and stimulus packages on offer. Furthermore, opposition to the implementation of Dodd-Frank has been enormous. Lobbying by the financial services industry to soften the legislation's actual regulatory bite has been massive, judging by the amount of money being spent by the industry on lobbying. In 2012, the top five consumer protection groups defending Dodd-Frank sent 20 lobbyists to Capitol Hill, while the top five finance industry groups trying to weaken, delay, and dismantle it sent 406 lobbyists.[43] The paradox, then, is that while evidence is mounting that neoliberalism does not work, many policy makers seem reluctant to abandon it permanently despite their short-term flirtations with alternative policy paradigms. This is unfortunate because the future looks grim. Attendees at the 2013 annual IMF research conference listened to Larry Summers, former economic advisor to Bill Clinton, George W. Bush, and Barack Obama and one of the architects of financial deregulation in the 1990s, explain that the advanced capitalist world may very well be in a permanent economic slump.[44] Bluntly, really serious reforms were not made, making it likely that future crises may well occur. Insofar as this reflects the failure of American neoliberalism, we wonder how long this ideological pillar of American hegemony can last.

---

[41] Krugman (2009); Stiglitz (2012); Wade and Veneroso (1998a, 1998b).
[42] Vezigiannidou (2013), p. 644.
[43] Rivlin (2013).
[44] Krugman (2013).

All of this is to stress an increasing precariousness of American power. But there is another way of looking at it, already mentioned when discussing the crisis of the euro. The United States exited the financial crisis in much better condition than did Europe. The initial injection of nearly $1 trillion dollars has been followed by extensive printing of money, through the quantitative easing program of the Federal Reserve. Equally important has been the determination to stress test banks and to make them get rid of risky assets or recapitalize their balance sheets. These policies have succeeded. Growth in the United States is far more vigorous than it is in Europe, and it remains the safe haven for money in troubled time. At the time of writing, the United States has benefited significantly from the inflow of monies occasioned by the crisis in Ukraine.

We wish to turn to a final issue, increasing income inequality, addressing it in an equally divided manner, at least in descriptive terms—for, in normative terms we are at one in wishing for an increase in equality. The facts themselves are stark and astonishing. By the early 2000s the richest 20 percent of American households received about 8.5 times more income (after taxes and government benefits) than the poorest 20 percent of households, which was worse than the other advanced capitalist countries. In Japan and Scandinavia, for instance, this gap was only half as large as it was in the United States.[45] This was not unrelated to American-style nationalist tensions—that is, tensions over race. In 2010, the median family income for African-Americans and Hispanics was only 59 percent and 69 percent, respectively, of the median family income of white families. The poverty rates for African-Americans and Hispanics were more than two and a half times greater than they were for whites. Problems of inequality grew worse in the wake of the 2008 financial crisis, thanks to persistently high rates of unemployment, which reduced incomes at the bottom, and the dramatic rebound of the stock market, which boosted incomes at the top.

Powerful arguments suggest that rising income inequality undermines national economic competitiveness by compromising economic efficiency. Cross-national research indicates that countries with lower levels of inequality are those with more generous income redistribution schemes involving both taxation and social spending.[46] We have already noted that greater inequality is associated with poorer educational performance. There is an equivalent link to higher rates of illness in society and therefore to absenteeism and poor productivity at work, both factors likely to undermine economic competitiveness. Analyses of the advanced capitalist countries show too that as income inequality rises, so do such social problems as crime, teen pregnancy, and illiteracy.[47] The United States fares particularly badly in these international comparisons. Poor literacy obviously undermines national economic performance insofar as we are moving toward a knowledge-based economy. Rising crime and teen pregnancy rates tend to divert government spending from potentially more productive investments toward other purposes, such as police and public safety, supporting prisons, and supporting single-

---

[45]Mishel et al. (2012), p. 161, 405; Wilkinson and Pickett (2009), p. 17.
[46]Brady 2009; Kenworthy 2010; Wilkinson and Pickett (2009).
[47]Wilkinson and Pickett (2009).

parent families, many of which are the result of teens having children out of wedlock. Inequality is of course partly the result of tax cuts for the rich, and attention needs to be given to the consequences of declining state revenues. Lost revenue makes it hard to sustain the educational and infrastructural investments necessary to maintain let alone improve economic competitiveness, especially when economic growth is lackluster as it has been for much of the last 30 years.[48] Finally, growing inequality helps destabilize politics in ways described above that lead to political gridlock and its associated problems. Indeed, as the middle class has been squeezed financially in the United States, it has become susceptible to just the sort of political extremism expressed by the Tea Party movement as well as those who fly the nationalist flag and complain about immigration.[49] All these factors are causing problems and will cause further problems for the United States.

It may be that there is another side to the picture, repulsive though it is in large part. One can imagine a society with high levels of inequality and poverty in which the government pursues policies that mitigate the political instability that inequality and poverty might breed. Roman emperors trumpeted the benefits of bread and circuses. The American system has added policies that result in high rates of incarceration particularly for poor, young men from minority groups—precisely those people most at risk of unemployment in the US labor market. Indeed, the rate of incarceration in the United States is roughly ten times greater than in Europe. Estimates suggest that by jailing those most likely to have trouble finding jobs, incarceration policies shave off as much as 2 percent from the official unemployment rate.[50] Still more important is the need to remember that capitalism can be run by different political systems, as we saw in the last chapter. Perhaps it is the case that a really advanced industrial economy may depend on the extraordinarily innovative brains of the few rather than the social solidarity of the many, upon Silicon Valley rather than upon Detroit.

Conclusion

We warned the reader that there would be two sides to our analysis of the United States, and we have certainly kept our word. On the one hand, there can be no doubt but that the United States has enormous reserves of strength. It retains military power, is threatened by no one, and has the possibility of downsizing some of its ill thought out escapades. It retains considerable economic power, both at the higher end of the product cycle and in finance, and its relationship with emerging markets is not necessarily antagonistic. On the other hand, hegemonic powers may yet be undermined through internal political stalemate, through failure to adapt to changing circumstances. We have listed many instances of this type of problem and now add one more—not least as it links domestic

---

[48]Stiglitz (2012).
[49]Lepore (2013); Wilkinson and Pickett (2009).
[50]Campbell (2010); Western and Beckett (1999).

politics to international affairs. The Obama administration has tried to change the IMF by giving China, Brazil, India, and other emerging economic powers more influence over its policies, so as to integrate them more closely to a revised world order. Republicans in Congress have blocked these efforts claiming that the United States cannot afford to pay for the $315 million it would take to make the rebalancing work properly. According to one former Treasury official, Congress's inaction is "a major blow to U.S. credibility around the world, with ominous consequences for the future of international economic, financial, and political cooperation .... In the future, the United States will be less trusted to implement international agreements in this and other areas."[51]

We recognize that we have raised more questions than we have answered. But so much is in flux at this moment that it is hard to be sure which way things are headed. Perhaps we may be allowed to emerge from description, a field in which we have been divided, to offer some prescriptions that we share. To begin with, please note that we are not urging protectionism as a response to the economic challenges posed by the emerging powers. History shows that protectionism can wreak all sorts of havoc in the world, whilst trade competition has done much to spur innovation. Besides, there are better ways to deal with the decline of good manufacturing jobs in America and the problems of wage stagnation and rising inequality that this incurs. Transfer payments is one option if done properly, such as through the earned income tax credit and the provision of universal health care, an option that is not nearly as expensive and considerably more beneficial than conservatives argue, particularly if it is linked to spending on skill formation and training, areas where the United States has slipped significantly during the last decade relative to other advanced countries. Such programs can easily be funded by modestly taxing high-income earners and by taxing profits held by US corporations overseas.[52] Of course, this returns us to the question of political stalemate. It is hard to see this changing, but one remembers Churchill's comment that the United States does the right thing but only when the hands of the clock are near to midnight.

Finally, let us reiterate a comment made about foreign policy. The geopolitical power of the United States trumped, probably mistakenly, the power that it could have exercised in the market place. Heroism in the Middle East took pride of place over trade. The costs to America in blood and treasure have been significant. So too has been the cost in soiled international reputation within the region as well as outside it, depending on the intervention in question. Prescriptively, it would make sense for the United States to take geopolitics out of economic matters, especially because it is weaning itself from fossil fuels from that part of the world. One can be engaged with the world with considerable effect without dominating it in this manner. Hegemony can be leadership rather than imperialism.

---

[51]Weisman (2014).

[52]Kenworthy (2013) has much to say on this subject.

CONCLUSION

We have argued that a proper understanding of our world must entail an analysis of power relations within and between states even in this era of economic globalization. Power has economic, political, and ideological elements, and it can be exercised coercively or created by a collectivity. Institutions freeze power relations in different ways and in different times and places. But historical change is so pervasive that what had seemed permanent often proves to be transitory, leading to the creation of new combinations designed for altered conditions. How could any of this be otherwise? After all, the interactions between states have helped structure the world throughout much of human history. We see no reason to believe that this will change.

We have shown that the key functions of the modern state as a genetic type—order, security, and belonging—are now met in different ways. The weak states of the South barely manage to meet them at all: state and nation building are far from complete, with survival resting on the fact that interstate war has been all but ruled out by observance of the norm of non-intervention. In contrast, rising powers are building states, with some of them benefiting from pre-existing national solidarities. These states too are fairly blessed by geopolitical security, based on the alliances created at the end of World War II. Much of the future will depend on the maintenance of such alliances, given that trade and prosperity depend upon a background of pre-existing geopolitical order. It is hard to be sure about the ultimate direction of some of these polities. Are democratic institutions needed to create political stability, something which would help India and Brazil—or, put differently, will the authoritarian rising powers, above all China, suffer at some point because of their inability to decompress so that centralized power will politicize social movements which will then take on the state? In contrast, much of the North looks stable, with its various sub-species still very much in existence. But this social world may decline in significance, not least as rising powers will eventually take a larger place at the seats of the great international institutions. We have insisted that the position of the United States will determine much, although the two of us see slightly different futures for that great power.

We can usefully end with some final reflections going a little beyond what has been said. The first matter of concern is that of nationalism, the force in the modern world that has proved to have greater teeth than class conflict, its putative rival. Europe has become a zone of peace, thankfully, but one should resist European self-satisfaction when speaking about nationalism. European liberalism is less impressive when one remembers that many states are liberal, thanks to the efforts of Hitler and Stalin, who removed their nationalities problems. The dilemma of scale and nation that concerned us so much in our first chapter is of course now faced by the European Union. There is everything to be said for the messy way in which it has become an Austro-Hungary that has worked; one hopes that it can remain, as Count Taaffe had it for the Hapsburgs, in a state of "bearable dissatisfaction." But one has to remember that nationalism is a labile force; it looks to be changing its character once again. The Danish vote on the euro pitted two views of national identity against each other: every element of the elite was in favor of joining, with eventual rejection being entirely nativist. To be a European citizen requires facility in several languages, allowing for career and geographical mobility.[1] There is ever more evidence that those lacking these skills resent Europe and wish integration to go no further.

Far more impressive than Europe is the wonderful fact that crucial parts of the world have found a route to the modern world that does not involve copying the disasters of the European past. What is most striking about India is its ability to create a state-nation rather than a nation-state. Indian leaders in the years before independence were aware of the problems of diversity and sought to accommodate them. It would have been immensely difficult to homogenize all of India, not least as Indian civil servants had cultural capital through their knowledge of English. Accordingly, as we explained previously, it was agreed that there would be two state languages, English and Hindi.[2] If one's state was Hindi-speaking, then one only needed two languages. But three were required if one's state was not Hindi-speaking and a fourth if one came from a minority in such a state. This linguistic regime seems to work in India, allowing for different peoples to live together under the same political roof. It is important to note that linguistic regimes of this type are not confined to India, with English serving as "neutral-speak" in several African countries. But there are of course other factors at work in the Indian case. For one thing, there is a structural skeleton to the Indian state—its army, its bureaucratic tradition, and the fact that an element of shared national identity arose from a common struggle against the British. For another, the Indian polity has shown itself to be flexible and liberal in diverse ways going beyond language. One striking example is the way in which pressures for secession in Tamil Nadu were diffused by the granting of varied political and cultural rights—in stark contrast to the situation in Sri Lanka, where homogenizing politics by the Sinhalese elite led to a civil war. The fact that there are areas of dissidence within India, above all in Kashmir, proves the point in question: those are the areas where India is, so to speak, not true to itself—illiberal in ways that we know all too well.[3]

In contrast, there is much to be said for worrying about the situation in China where the alternative route is being taken—of homogenization though forcible assimilation and the diluting of minority populations by the traditional method of moving in large numbers of the majority population. One worry is that this route may breed violent response, the desire for secession that was present in key parts of Europe in modern times, above all in Tibet, Hong Kong, and Taiwan. One can note in this regard that

---

[1]Laitin (1997).
[2]Laitin (1992).
[3]Stepan et al. (2011).

the situation in China is in fact rather different from some of the cases noted above. Han Chinese are a massive majority, and it may well be that over time they can have their way; homogenization may yet work. A second worry is greater. There is a sense in which contemporary China resembles Wilhelmine Germany. The regime worries about it's legitimacy, and it may yet seek to enhance it by playing the nationalist card. Certainly, new middle-class elements exist, above all the massive student population, which wish for a more aggressive policy on the part of their state, believing in its right to a central place in world affairs. Eyre Crowe's famous memorandum suggested that Germany, for whatever reasons, wished to break up the British empire so as to supplant it. Thomas Sanderson opposed this view in an interesting memorandum of February 21, 1907, in which he saw Germany as "a helpful though somewhat exacting friend," adding that, "it is altogether contrary to reason that Germany should wish to quarrel with us."[4] Germany was prospering in 1914 within the rules of the world order of the times and looked set to prosper much more. The same is true of China today. One hopes that the result of developments in the two countries will differ, with Chinese behavior to this point justifying worry rather than fear.

A final point concerns the fact that so many have been killed in the putatively peaceful postwar world in civil wars, very often fueled by ethnic strife—the end result in large part of European colonialism. But there are reasons to hope here, reasons to think that links between nationalism and war may weaken—and this beyond the current diminution in the numbers of such conflicts. One can at least hope that the strict version of the nation-state—each state with its own culture and each culture with its own state—may be avoided. Design may help. Much more important is a background factor, a diminution in the intensity of great power rivalry and of their involvement in much of the rest of the world. Relative geopolitical calm may allow states to manage their nations in a less unitary and homogenous manner. This is not to say, however, that great power rivalries have fully ended. Russia and the United States are heavily involved in the civil war now taking place in Syria. Russia backs Assad with weapons while the United States and other countries are providing support to various members of the opposition. Proxy wars among the great powers may have subsided but they have not disappeared.

A second issue deserving further consideration is neoliberalism. This ideology has had an increasing impact on economic policymaking nationally and internationally since the late 1970s. Its intellectual origins were in the 1940s, but it gained political traction in the United States and Britain during the 1980s under Reagan and Thatcher, respectively, and spread in varying degree to a number of other countries after that. It also morphed into the so-called Washington Consensus—the template that the IMF and World Bank used for international development. The consequences have not been good. Russia and the East European countries flirted with neoliberalism in the early 1990s; most back tracked after a few years because it contributed to soaring inequality, deteriorating

---

[4]Sanderson (1928), pp. 430–431.

public health, political instability, and a host of other political and economic problems. Neoliberal policies contributed to the 1997 Asian financial crisis as well. Most recently and most importantly, neoliberalism was largely responsible for removing regulation of the financial system, a major cause of the 2008 financial crisis. This brought the world economy to its knees, nearly leading to a second Great Depression. The world has still not recovered fully from the 2008 crisis. Growth rates and unemployment rates in many of the affected countries have yet to return to pre-crisis levels and it is not clear when they will. Moreover, the austerity policies adopted in many European countries that were based on neoliberal prescriptions and that were supposed to pull these countries out of recession have signally failed to do so.[5]

The irony here is twofold. First, the countries that allegedly pioneered neoliberalism—the United States and Britain—actually never embraced it in real terms as much as they did in ideological ones. Reagan's efforts at neoliberal tax, welfare, and regulatory reform were never as draconian as the rhetoric of the day suggested. Thatcher's attack on the welfare state was never as successful as many people assumed.[6] Those in other countries who advocated neoliberalism based on their understanding of the United States and Britain sought to mimic something that was as much myth as it was reality. Second, despite the impressive failures of neoliberalism, it is not clear that neoliberalism's heyday has passed. This is especially surprising because in some countries, policymakers appeared to have thrown neoliberalism out the window after 2008 in favor of other policies. Both the Bush and Obama administrations implemented a wide-ranging set of fiscal, monetary, and regulatory policies that seemed to signal a return to Keynesianism. Nevertheless, there are still politicians and economists in many countries who remain committed to neoliberalism. The reasons for this are complex.[7] But it remains an open question how much longer policymakers' devotion to neoliberalism will last and how much evidence it will take to convince them that it is deeply flawed. One notes the relative failure of attempts to regulate financial markets. In consequence, it is likely that there will be further disruptions of the world economy.

A third set of reflections concerns the United States. The self-image of this great power is one that privileges society rather than the state, somewhat oddly in our view, given the sheer power of its polity. This matters: the United States has been loath to recognize the benefits of nationalism in the world as a whole, whilst its preference for societal forces explains its endorsement of neoliberal policies that make state building in the South so very difficult. Most importantly, we want to reiterate and amplify a point already made. The United States differs from other countries in the North in having a freedom of action derived fundamentally from it not being dependent on the rest of the world. The country has often been attracted to heroic rather than to trading policies. This has often caused disaster, most obviously in the Middle East and in South East Asia. Hence, we have stressed the importance of thinking anew about geopolitics.

---

[5]Blyth (2013).
[6]Bunch (2009); Pierson (1994).
[7]Crouch (2011).

The size of the market of the United States and its allies is a source of immense power. Countries with resources need to sell them if they are to prosper; purchasing even at higher prices may well be a better policy than the imposition of costly controls. Heroism reached something of an apogee in the political romanticism that dominated the administration of Bush the Younger. The retreat from excess is surely to be welcomed. This is not, however, to encourage isolationism and protectionism. Rather, we suggest a little more modesty on the part of this great power, a continuation of its security systems both in Europe and in Asia freed from impossible expansionist dreams.

We turn finally to the most important issue for the future of the world, and do so with great fears at the back of our mind. An initial fear is simple. Capitalist societies have very often been stable as the result of economic growth, an increase in the size of the economy sufficient to buy off discontent. We find it very hard to imagine liberal polities without such growth and have implicitly held societies that create it to be successful. Moreover, basic morality leads us to hope that the vast numbers of mankind living in poverty will gain the benefits that we enjoy. To entertain these hopes brings us face to face with the hideous prospect that the ensuing global warming may threaten humanity with extinction. But even before this happens, it helps spawn more violent and dangerous weather patterns including severe blizzards, hurricanes, tornados, floods, and droughts. It also melts the polar ice caps, which raises sea levels and exacerbates the possibilities for major flooding around the world. In 2005, the ten cities with the highest population exposure to such flooding were scattered around the globe: Mumbai, Guangzhou, Shanghai, Miami, Ho Chi Minh City, Kolkata, New York, Osaka-Koba, Alexandria, and New Orleans. The value of assets at risk from flooding in these cities alone was estimated to be $3 trillion—roughly 5 percent of world GDP.[8] Of course, these are all major ports, so flooding would also dramatically disrupt international trade and raise the costs further. And it is not hard to imagine the disruptive toll such disasters would take on people's daily lives.

We are not complete pessimists. Many nation-states have recognized and started to grapple with problems of air and water pollution as they have emerged. Some countries have also worked hard to conserve energy by developing wind, solar, biomass, and other alternative energy sources. Even nuclear power, which has long been the bane of many environmentalists, is becoming more attractive in part because the technology of nuclear power is becoming safer and is cleaner in terms of global warming than fossil fuels. This is not to say that nuclear power is a panacea. There are still serious problems regarding the long-term disposal of highly toxic radioactive waste from commercial nuclear reactors that lasts thousands of years. Nonetheless, our concern with state power does lead us to two very serious fears.

The first is simple. Really effective policies to deal with global warming must be international, created and managed by the world as a whole. Our world of states makes

---

[8]OECD (2007).

this impossible, at least at the present time. The United States would like China to emit less greenhouse gases, a view considered by the Chinese to be the purest hypocrisy, designed to deprive them of a decent way of life—and an insulting one at that, given the damage done by the relatively small population of the United States, in the past and today, to the planet. The attempt to bring these two great powers together to deal with this issue at the Copenhagen Conference in December 2009 was manifestly a failure. What one notices now in the United States is that environmental policies are losing rather than gaining ground: the "fracking" revolution might grow the economy, but it is a disaster for the world. Moreover, a vocal minority of politicians and others deny the human causes of climate change. China takes climate change more seriously as it has to, given the horrors of pollution in its capital city. But China remains poor, and all estimates suggest that its continuing growth will do much to harm the planet.

The second fear involves the question of territorial size. The desire for size at the end of the nineteenth century, for secure markets and sources of supply, led to inter-imperial conflict. We have done better in an interdependent world, trusting to market forces for our prosperity. One wonders if this will continue. Might not extensive territory blessed with the full panoply of resources necessary for prosperity become attractive once again? A country so favored might become a fortress, able to exclude the mass of migrants likely to flow from an ecological catastrophe. We need cooperation between states, but that might not be our fate.

REFERENCES

Adler, A. and M. Barnett (eds) 1998. *Security Communities*. Cambridge: Cambridge University Press.

African Economic Outlook. 2014. http://www.africaneconomicoutlook.org/en/statistics/ (Accessed May 2014).

Alamgir, J. 2003. "Managing Openness in India: The Social Construction of a Globalist Narrative." in *States in the Global Economy*, edited by Linda Weiss, pp. 225–244. New York, NY: Cambridge University Press.

Alpert, D. 2013. *The Age of Oversupply*. New York, NY: Penguin.

Amin, S. 1976. *Unequal Development*. New York, NY: Monthly Review Press.

Anderson, B. 1983. *Imagined Communities*. London: Verso.

Anderson, P. 2009. *The New Old World*. London: Verso.

Aron, R. 1957. *La Tragédie Algérienne*, Paris: Plon.

———. 1979. *The Imperial Republic*. London: Weidenfeld and Nicolson.

Ash, T.G. 2004. *Free World: America, Europe and the Surprising Future of the West*. New York, NY: Random House.

Babb, S. 2001. *Managing Mexico*. Princeton, NJ: Princeton University Press.

Bang, P. 2008. *The Roman Bazaar: A Comparative Study of Trade and Markets in a Tributary Empire*. Cambridge: Cambridge University Press.

Baran, P. 1957. *The Political Economy of Growth*. New York, NY: Monthly Review Press.

Barnett, S., A. Myrvoda and M. Nabar. 2012. "Sino-Spending." *Finance and Development*, September, Vol. 49, No. 3, International Monetary Fund. http://www.imf.org/external/pubs/ft/fandd/2012/09/barnett.htm (Accessed December 2013).

Bates, R. 2008. *When Things Fell Apart: State Failure in Late-Century Africa*. Cambridge: Cambridge University Press.

Berghahn, V. 2001. *America and the Intellectual Cold Wars in Europe*. Princeton, NJ: Princeton University Press.

Block, F. 2008. "Swimming Against the Current: The Rise of a Hidden Developmental State in the United States." *Politics and Society* 36: 169–206.

Bluestone, B. and B. Harrison. 1982. *The Deindustrialization of America*. New York, NY: Basic Books.

Blyth, M. 2013. *Austerity: The History of a Dangerous Idea*. New York, NY: Oxford University Press.

Bova, R. 1991. "Political Dynamics of the Post-Communist Transition: A Comparative Perspective." *World Politics* 44(1): 113–138.

Brady, D. 2009. *Rich Democracies, Poor People*. New York, NY: Oxford University Press.

Breslin, S. 2013. "China and the Global Order; Signaling Threat of Friendship?" *International Affairs* 89(3): 615–634.

Brooks, S.G. 2005. *Producing Security*. Princeton, NJ: Princeton University Press.

Brooks, S.G., G.J. Ikenberry and W.C. Wohlforth. 2012. "Don't Come Home, America: The Case Against Retrenchment." *International Security* 37(3): 7–51.

Buera, F. and J. Kaboski. 2009. "The Rise of the Service Economy." National Bureau of Economic Research Working Paper 14822. Cambridge: NBER. http://www.nber.org/papers/w14822.pdf?new_window=1 (Accessed January 2014).

References

Bunch, W. 2009. *Tear Down This Myth: How the Reagan Legacy Has Distorted Our Politics and Haunts Our Future*. New York, NY: Free Press.

Burges, S.W. 2013. "Brazil as a Bridge Between Old and New Powers?" *International Affairs* 89(3): 577–594.

Burke, P. 1986. "City-States." in *States in History*, edited by J.A. Hall, pp. 137–153. Oxford: Basil Blackwell.

Calmes, J. 2013. "A Dirty Secret Lurks in the Struggle Over a Fiscal 'Grand Bargain.'" *The New York Times*, November 19, A17.

Campbell, J.L. 2003. "States, Politics, and Globalization: Why Institutions Still Matter." in *The Nation State in Question*, edited by T.V. Paul, G. John Ikenberry and John A. Hall, pp. 234–259. Princeton, NJ: Princeton University Press.

———. 2004. *Institutional Change and Globalization*. Princeton, NJ: Princeton University Press.

———. 2005. "Fiscal Sociology in an Age of Globalization: Comparing Tax Regimes in Advanced Capitalist Countries." in *The Economic Sociology of Capitalism*, edited by Victor Nee and Richard Swedberg, pp. 391–418. Princeton, NJ: Princeton University Press.

———. 2010. "Neoliberalism's Penal and Debtor States: A Rejoinder to Loïc Wacquant." *Theoretical Criminology* 14(1): 59–73.

———. 2011. "The U.S. Financial Crisis: Lessons for Theories of Institutional Complementarity." *Socio-Economic Review* 9(2): 211–234.

Campbell, J.L., J.R. Hollingsworth and L.N. Lindberg (eds) 1991. *Governance of the American Economy*. New York, NY: Cambridge University Press.

Campbell, J.L. and O.K. Pedersen. 2014. *The National Origins of Policy Ideas: Knowledge Regimes in the United States, France, Germany, and Denmark*. Princeton, NJ: Princeton University Press.

Centeno, M. 2002. *Blood and Debt: War and the Nation-State in Latin America*. University Park: Pennsylvania State University.

Centeno, M. and J. Cohen. 2010. *Global Capitalism*. Cambridge: Polity.

Center on Budget and Policy Priorities. 2013. *Policy Basics: Where Do Our Federal Tax Dollars Go?* Washington, DC: Center on Budget and Policy Priorities. http://www.cbpp.org/cms/?fa=view&id=1258 (Accessed January 2014).

Center for Responsive Politics. 2013. Opensecrets.org. http://www.opensecrets.org/ (Accessed November 2013).

Chandler, A.D., Jr. 1992. "The Emergence of Managerial Capitalism." in *The Sociology of Economic Life*, edited by Mark Granovetter and Richard Swedberg, pp. 131–158. Boulder, CO: Westview.

Citizenship and Immigration Canada. 2013. *News Release—Canada Welcomes Record Number of Immigrants, Visitors and Students from China in 2012*. Ottawa: Government of Canada. http://www.cic.gc.ca/english/department/media/releases/2013/2013-03-04c.asp (Accessed March 4, 2013).

Collier, P. 2000. "Economic Causes of Civil War and their Implications for Policy." in *Managing Global Chaos: Sources of and Responses to International Conflict*, edited by C. Crocker, F.O. Hampson and P.R. Aall. Washington, DC: US Institute for Peace.

Corbridge, S., G. Williams, M. Srivastava and R. Veron. 2005. *Seeing the State: Governance and Governmentality in India*. Cambridge: Cambridge University Press.

Crone, P. 1986. "The Tribe and the State." in *States in History*, edited by J.A. Hall, pp. 48–77. Oxford: Basil Blackwell.

Crouch, C. 2011. *The Strange Non-Death of Neoliberalism*. London: Polity.

Crowe, E. 1928. "Memorandum on the Present State of British Relations with France and Germany." in *British Documents on the Origins of the War, 1898–1914*. Volume Three: *The Testing of the Entne, 1904–6*, edited by G.P. Gooch and H. Temperley. London: Her Majesty's Stationery Office.

Darwin, J. 2007. *After Tamerlane: The Rise and Fall of Global Empires, 1400–2000*. London: Penguin.

Deutsch, K., S.A. Burrell, R.A. Kann, M. Lee, M. Lichterman, L. Francis, F.L. Loewenheim and R. van Wagenen. 1957. *Political Community in the North Atlantic Area: International Organization in the Light of Historical Experience*. Princeton, NJ: Princeton University Press.

Dezalay, Y. and B. Garth. 2002. *The Internationalization of Palace Wars*. Chicago, IL: University of Chicago Press.

Duina, F. 1999. *Harmonizing Europe: Nation-States within the Common Market*. Albany: State University of New York Press.

Easterly, W. 2008. "Foreign Aid Goes Military!" *New York Review of Books*, December 4, 51–54.

Economist. 2005. "The puny economic powerhouse.". *The Economist*, December 10.

———. 2009. "Failed states: Fixing a broken world." *The Economist*, January 21, 65–67.

———. 2012. "To Each, Not According to His Needs." December 15. http://www.economist.com/news/finance-and-economics/21568423-new-survey-illuminates-extent-chinese-income-inequality-each-not (Accessed December 2013).

———. 2013a. "When Giants Slow Down." *The Economist*, July 27, 20–22.

———. 2013b. "The Gated Globe." *The Economist*. October 12, 1–20.

———. 2013c. "A Man of Some of the People." *The Economist*, December 14, 31–33.

———. 2013d. "Sweeping Up." *The Economist*. December 14, 49.

———. 2013e. "A Holy Mess: Kidnapping in Nigeria is Out of Hand." *The Economist*, September 14.

———. 2014a. "Where Will the Rainbow End?" *The Economist*, May 3, 41–43.

———. 2014b. "Kidnappings in Nigeria: A Clueless Government." *The Economist*, May 10, 45–46.

———. 2014c. "Turkey's Economy: The Mask is Off." *The Economist*, January 2014.

Esping-Andersen, G. 1985. *Politics Against Markets: The Social Democratic Road to Power*. Princeton, NJ: Princeton University Press.

———. 1990. *The Three Worlds of Welfare Capitalism*. Princeton, NJ: Princeton University Press.

———. 1999. *Social Foundations of Postindustrial Economies*. New York, NJ: Oxford University Press.

Evans, P. 1995. *Embedded Autonomy: States and Industrial Transformation*. Princeton, NJ: Princeton University Press.

Fearon, J.D. and D.D. Laitin. 2003. "Ethnicity, Insurgency and Civil War." *American Political Science Review* 97(1): 75–90.

Financial Times Alphaville. 2013. "The Collapse of U.S. Infrastructure Spending." October 31. http://ftalphaville.ft.com/2013/10/31/1683112/the-collapse-of-us-infrastructure-spending-charted/ (Accessed January 2014).

Fligstein, N. 2001. *Euroclash: The EU, European Identity, and the Future of Europe*. Oxford: Oxford University Press.

———. 2008. *The Architecture of Markets*. Princeton, NJ: Princeton University Press.

Fourcade-Gourinchas, M. 2006. "The Construction of a Global Profession: The Transnationalization of Economics." *American Journal of Sociology* 112(1): 145–194.

Fourcade-Gourinchas, M. and S. Babb. 2002. "The Rebirth of the Liberal Creed: Paths to Neoliberalism in Four Countries." *American Journal of Sociology* 108(3): 533–579.

Gellner, E.A. 1967. "Democracy and Industrialization." *European Journal of Sociology* 8(1): 47–70.

———. 1969. *Saints of the Atlas*. London: Weidenfeld and Nicolson.

———. 1983. *Nations and Nationalism*. Oxford: Blackwell.

Gereffi, G. 1994. "The International Economy and Economic Development." in *The Handbook of Economic Sociology*, edited by Neil Smelser and Richard Swedberg, pp. 206–233. Princeton, NJ: Princeton University Press.

References

Ghani, A. and C. Lockhart. 2008. *Fixing Failed States: A Framework for Rebuilding a Fractured World*. Oxford: Oxford University Press.

Gilpin, R. 1981. *War and Change in World History*. Cambridge: Cambridge University Press.

Goldstone, J., R. Bates, T.R. Gurr, M. Lustik, M.G. Marshall, J. Ulfelder and M. Woodward. 2005. *A Global Forecasting Model of Political Instability*. McLean, VA: State Failure Task Force, SAIC.

Guéhenno, J. 1993. *The End of the Nation-State*. Minneapolis: University of Minnesota Press.

Guillén, M. 2001. *The Limits of Convergence: Globalization and Organizational Change in Argentina, South Korea, and Spain*. Princeton, NJ: Princeton University Press.

Guillén, M. and E. García-Canal. 2010. *The New Multinationals*. New York, NY: Cambridge University Press.

Guillén, M. and E. Ontiveros. 2012. *Global Turning Points: Understanding the Challenges for Business in the 21st Century*. New York, NY: Cambridge University Press.

Gulati, R. and M. Gargiulo. 1999. "Where Do Interorganizational Networks Come From?" *American Journal of Sociology* 104(5): 1439–1493.

Habermas, J. 2005. *Time of Transitions*. Cambridge: Polity.

Hall, J.A. 1985. *Powers and Liberties: The Causes and Consequences of the Rise of the West*. Oxford: Blackwell.

———. 1996. *International Orders*. Cambridge: Polity.

———. 2013. *The Importance of Being Civil: The Struggle for Political Decency*. Princeton, NJ: Princeton University Press.

Hall, J.A. and C. Lindholm. 1999. *Is America Breaking Apart?* Princeton, NJ: Princeton University Press.

Hall, J.A. and D. Zhao. 1994. "State Power and Patterns of Late Development: Resolving the Crisis of the Sociology of Development." *Sociology* 28(1): 211–230.

Hall, P. 1986. *Governing the Economy*. New York, NY: Oxford University Press.

Hall, P. and D. Soskice (eds) 2001. *Varieties of Capitalism*. New York, NY: Oxford University Press.

Halliday, T. and B. Carruthers. 2009. *Bankrupt: Global Lawmaking and Systemic Financial Crisis*. Stanford, CA: Stanford University Press.

Hamilton, D.S. and J.P. Quinlan. 2011. *The Transatlantic Economy, 2011*. Baltimore, MD: Center for Transatlantic Relations, Johns Hopkins University.

Hann, C. 2013. "Levels of Parochialism: Welsh-Eurasian Perspectives on a German-European Debate." *Comparativ* 23(4/5): 122–135.

Harris, G. 2013. "India's Upper House Approves Anticorruption Agency." *The New York Times*, December 17, A12.

Herbst, J. 2000. *States and Power in Africa: Comparative Lessons in Authority and Control*. Princeton, NJ: Princeton University Press.

———. 2004. "Let Them Fail: State Failure in Theory and Practice: Implications for Policy." in *When States Fail: Causes and Consequences*, edited by R. Rotberg, pp. 302–318. Princeton, NJ: Princeton University Press.

Heymann, J. and A. Earle. 2010. *Raising the Global Floor*. Stanford, CA: Stanford University Press.

Hobbes, T. 1982. *Leviathan*. New York, NY: Penguin.

Hopewell, K. 2013. "New Protagonists in Global Economic Governance: Brazilian Agribusiness at the WTO". *New Political Economy* 18(4): 603–623.

Horne, A. 1988. *Harold Macmillan. Volume One: 1894–1956*. New York, NY: Viking.

Howard, C. 1997. *The Hidden Welfare State: Tax Expenditures and Social Policy in the United States*. Princeton, NJ: Princeton University Press.

Ikenberry, J.G. 2002. *After Victory*. Princeton, NJ: Princeton University Press.

———. 2008. "The Rise of China and the Future of the West." *Foreign Affairs* 87(1): 23–37.

International Bank for Reconstruction and Development/World Bank. 2012. *Doing Business 2012*. Washington, DC: IBRC/World Bank.

International Monetary Fund. 2013. "IMF Releases Data on the Currency Composition of Foreign Exchange Reserves with Additional Data on Australian and Canadian Dollar Reserves." IMF Press Releases, June 28. http://www.imf.org/external/np/sec/pr/2013/pr13236.htm (Accessed November 2013).

Jackson, R.H. 1990. *Quasi-States: Sovereignty, International Relations and the Third World*. Cambridge: Cambridge University Press.

Janelli, R. 1993. *Making Capitalism: The Social and Cultural Construction of a South Korean Conglomerate*. Stanford, CA: Stanford University Press.

Jones, E. 2008. *Economic Adjustment and Political Transformation in Small States*. New York, NY: Oxford University Press.

Kagan, R. 2003. *Of Paradise and Power: America and Europe in the New World Order*. New York, NY: Knopf.

Kaiser, W. 2007. *Christian Democracy and the Making of the European Union*. Cambridge: Cambridge University Press.

Kato, J. 2003. *Regressive Taxation and the Welfare State*. New York, NY: Cambridge University Press.

Katzenstein, P. 1985. *Small States in World Markets*. Ithaca, NY: Cornell University Press.

———. 2005. *A World of Regions: Asia and Europe in the American Imperium*. Ithaca, NY: Cornell University Press.

Kenworthy, L. 2004. *Egalitarian Capitalism: Jobs, Incomes, and Growth in Affluent Countries*. New York, NY: Russell Sage.

———. 2010. "Institutions, Wealth, and Inequality." in *The Oxford Handbook of Comparative Institutional Analysis*, edited by Glenn Morgan, John L. Campbell, Colin Crouch, Ove K. Pedersen and Richard Whitley, pp. 399–420. New York, NY: Oxford University Press.

———. 2011. *Progress for the Poor*. New York, NY: Oxford University Press.

———. 2013. *Social Democratic America*. New York, NY: Oxford University Press.

Kerr, C., J.T. Dunlop, F. Barbison and C.A. Meyers. 1960. *Industrialism and Industrial Man*. Cambridge: Harvard University Press.

Kohli, A. 2004. *State-Directed Development: Political Power and Industrialization in the Global Periphery*. Cambridge: Cambridge University Press.

Krasner, S.D. 2005. "The Case for Shared Sovereignty." *Journal of Democracy* 16(1): 69–83.

Krugman, P. 2009. *The Return of Depression Economics and the Crisis of 2008*. New York, NY: Norton.

———. 2013. "A Permanent Slump?" *The New York Times*, November 18, A27.

Laitin, D.D. 1992. *Language Repertoires and State Construction in Africa*. Cambridge: Cambridge University Press.

———. 1997. "The Cultural Identities of a European State." *Politics and Society* 25(3): 277–302.

———. 2008. *Nations, States and Violence*. Oxford: Oxford University Press.

Lange, M. 2010. "State Formation, Consolidation, and the Security Challenge: Exploring the Causes of State Incapacity in South Asia." in *South Asia's Weak States and the Regional Insecurity Predicament*, edited by T.V. Paul. Stanford: Stanford University Press.

———. 2013. *Educations in Ethnic Violence*. New York, NY: Cambridge University Press.

———. 2015. "State Formation and Transformation in Africa and Asia: The Third Phase of State Expansion." in *The Oxford Handbook on the Transformations of States*, edited by S. Liebfried, E. Huber, M. Mange, J. Levy and J. Stephens. Oxford: Oxford University Press.

Lattimore, O. 1962. *Studies in Frontier History*. Oxford: Oxford University Press.

Lee, C.K. 2007. *Against the Law: Labor Protests in China's Rustbelt and Sunbelt*. Berkeley, CA: University of California Press.

References

Legrain, P. 2014. *European Spring: Why Our Economies and Politics Are in a Mess and How to Put Them Right.* London: CB Books.

Leonard, M. 2005. *Why Europe Will Run the 21st Century.* London: Fourth Estate.

Lepore, J. 2013. "Long Division: Measuring the Polarization of American Politics." *The New Yorker*, December 2, 75–79.

Lieven, D. 1999. "Dilemmas of Empire 1850–1918. Power, Territory, Identity." *Journal of Contemporary History* 34(2): 163–200.

Lundestad, G. 1986. "Empire by Invitation? The United States and Western Europe, 1945–52." *Journal of Peace Research* 23(3): 263–277.

Mabry, T. 2015. *Nationalism, Language and Islam.* Philadelphia: University of Pennsylvania Press.

Maier, Charles. 1981. "The Two Postwar eras and the Conditions for Stability in Twentieth Century Europe." *American Historical Review* 86(2): 327–352.

Mamdani, M. 2001. *When Victims Become Killers.* Princeton, NJ: Princeton University Press.

———. 2008. "Lessons of Zimbabawe." *London Review of Books*, December 4, 17–21.

Mann, M. 1984. "The Autonomous Power of the State: Its Origins, Mechanisms and Results." *Archives Europeennes de Sociologie* 15: 185–213.

———. 1986. *The Sources of Social Power. Volume One: From the Beginning to 1760AD.* Cambridge: Cambridge University Press.

———. 1993. *The Sources of Social Power. Volume Two: The Rise of Classes and Nation-States.* Cambridge: Cambridge University Press.

———. 2013. *The Sources of Social Power. Volume Three: Global Empires and Revolution, 1890–1945.* New York, NY: Cambridge University Press.

———. 2014. *The Sources of Social Power. Volume Four: Globalizations, 1945–2011.* New York, NY: Cambridge University Press.

Mann, M. and D. Riley. 2007. Explaining Macro-regional Trends in Global Income Inequalities, 1950–2000. *Socio-Economic Review* 5(1): 81–115.

Medrano, J.D. 2003. *Framing Europe: Attitudes to European Integration in Germany, Spain and the United Kingdom.* Princeton, NJ: Princeton University Press.

Miller, B. 2007. *States, Nations and Great Powers: The Sources of Regional War and Peace.* Cambridge: Cambridge University Press.

Milward, A. 1984. *The Reconstruction of Western Europe, 1945–51.* Berkeley, CA: University of California Press.

———. 1992. *The European Rescue of the Nation-State.* Berkeley, CA: University of California Press.

Mishel, L., J. Bivens, E. Gould and H. Shierholz. 2012. *The State of Working America.* 12th edition. Ithaca, NY: Cornell University Press.

Moravscik, A. 1998. *The Choice for Europe: Social Purpose and State Power from Messina to Maastricht.* Ithaca, NY: Cornell University Press.

Motyl, A.J. 2001. *Imperial Ends: The Decay, Collapse and Revival of Empires.* New York, NY: Columbia University Press.

Mowle, T. 2004. *Allies at Odds: The United States and the European Union.* Basingstoke: Macmillan.

Mudge, S. 2008. "What is Neoliberalism?" *Socio-Economic Review* 6(4): 703–731.

———. 2011. "What's Left of Leftism? Neoliberal Politics in Western Party Systems, 1945–2008." *Social Science History* 35(3): 337–380.

Narlikar, A. 2013. "India Rising: Responsible to Whom?" *International Affairs* 89(3): 595–614.

Nef, J.U. 1963. *War and Human Progress: An Essay on the Rise of Industrial Civilization.* New York, NY: Norton.

New York Times. 2013. "Why Students Do Better Overseas." December 18, A28.

Nolan, P. 2012. *Is China Buying the World?* Cambridge: Polity Press.

North Atlantic Treaty Organization. 2014. *Secretary General's Annual Report 2013*. Brussels: NATO.

OECD. 2006. *OECD Factbook, 2006*. Paris: OECD.

———. 2013. "Real Gross Domestic Product—Forecasts." November 19. Paris: OECD. http://www.oecd-ilibrary.org/economics/real-gross-domestic-product-forecasts_gdp-kusd-gr-table-en (Accessed January 2014).

O'Leary, B. 2001. "An Iron Law of Nationalism and Federation? A (Neo-Diceyan) Theory of the Necessity of a Staatsvolk." *Nations and Nationalism* 7(3): 273–296.

Ó Riain, S. 2014. *The Rise and Fall of Ireland's Celtic Tiger: Liberalism, Boom and Bust*. New York, NY: Cambridge University Press.

Ornston, D. 2012. *When Small States Make Big Leaps*. Ithaca, NY: Cornell University Press.

Palier, B. and K. Thelen. 2012. "Dualization and Institutional Competitiveness: Industrial Relations, Labor Market and Welfare State Changes in France and Germany." in *The Age of Dualization: Structures, Policies, Politics and Divided Outcomes*, edited by Patrick Emmenegger, Silja Häusermann, Bruno Palier and Martin Seeleib-Kaiser, pp. 201–225. New York, NJ: Oxford University Press.

Pauly, L. 1997. *Who Elected the Bankers?* Ithaca, NY: Cornell University Press.

Pederson, O.K. 2006. "Negotiated Economy: Corporatism and Beyond." in *National Identity and Varieties of Capitalism*, edited by John L. Campbell, John A. Hall and Ove K. Pedersen, pp. 245–270. Montreal: McGill-Queen's University Press.

———. 2011. *Konkurrencestaten*. Copenhagen: Hans Reitzels Forlag.

Piore, M. and C. Sabel. 1984. *The Second Industrial Divide*. New York, NY: Basic Books.

Polanyi, K. 1944. *The Great Transformation*. Boston, MA: Beacon.

Pond, E. 2004. *Friendly Fire: The Near-Death of the Transatlantic Alliance*. Washington, DC: Brookings.

Posner, D.N. 2004a. "Measuring Ethnic Fractionalization in Africa." *American Journal of Political Science* 48(4): 849–863.

———. 2004b. "Civil Society and the Reconstruction of Failed States." in *When States Fail: Causes and Consequences*, edited by R. Rotberg, pp. 237–255. Princeton, NJ: Princeton University Press.

Powell, W.W. 1987. "Hybrid Organizational Arrangements." *California Management Review* 30(1): 67–87.

Prasad, E. 2014. *The Dollar Trap: How the U.S. Dollar Tightened Its Grip on Global Finance*. Princeton, NJ: Princeton University Press.

Rashid, A. 2008. *Descent Into Chaos: The United States and the Failure of Nation Building in Pakistan, Afghanistan and Central Asia*. New York, NY: Viking.

Rattner, S. 2013. "Congress Avoids Reality, Again." *The New York Times*, December 11, A29.

Reinhart, C. and K. Rogoff. 2008. "We Need an International Regulator." *Financial Times*, November 19.

Rich, F. 2006. *The Greatest Story Ever Told*. New York, NY: Penguin.

Rifkin, J. 2004. *The European Dream*. Cambridge: Polity.

Riga, L. 2012. *The Bolsheviks and the Russian Empire*. Cambridge: Cambridge University Press.

Ripsman, N. 2005. "Two Stages of Transition from a Region of War to a Region of Peace: Realist Transition and Liberal Endurance." *International Studies Quarterly* 49(4): 669–693.

Rivlin, G. 2013. "Outnumbered by Bank Lobbyists." *The Nation*, May 20. http://www.thenation.com/article/174113/how-wall-street-defanged-dodd-frank (Accessed November 2013).

Rodgers, D. 1998. *Atlantic Crossings*. Cambridge: Harvard University Press.

Rotberg, R. (ed.) 2003. *State Failure and State Weakness in a Time of Terror*. Washington, DC: Brookings Institution Press and the World Peace Foundation.

———. 2004. *When States Fail: Causes and Consequences*. Princeton, NJ: Princeton University Press.

References

Roy, W. 1997. *Socializing Capital: The Rise of the Large Industrial Corporation in America*. Princeton, NJ: Princeton University Press.

Ruggie, J. 1982. "International Regimes, Transactions and Change: Embedded Liberalism in the Postwar Economic Order." *International Organization* 36(2): 379–415.

Samuels, R. 1987. *The Business of the Japanese State*. Ithaca, NY: Cornell University Press.

Sanderson, T. 1928. "Memorandum." in *British Documents on the Origins of the War, 1898–1914, Volume Three: The Testing of the Entne, 1904–6*, edited by G.P. Gooch and H. Temperley. London: Her Majesty's Stationery Office.

Schaper, T. and K. Schaeper. 1998. *Cowboys and Gentlemen: Rhodes Scholars, Oxford and the Creation of an American Elite*. Leamington Spa: Berg.

Scheidel, W. 2013. "Studying the State." in *The Oxford Handbook of the Ancient State*, edited by P. Bang and W. Scheidel. Oxford: Oxford University Press.

Schlosser, E. 2013. *Command and Control: Nuclear Weapons, the Damascus Accident, and the Illusion of Safety*. New York, NY: Penguin.

Scott, J.C. 1998. *Seeing Like a State: How Certain Schemes to Improve the Human Condition Have Failed*. New Haven, CT: Yale University Press.

Sen, A. 1981. *Poverty and Famines: An Essay on Entitlement and Deprivation*. Oxford: Clarendon Press.

Shaw, G.B. 1907. *John Bull's Other Island, and Major Barbara. Also How He Lied to Her Husband*. London: Constable.

Simmons, B., F. Dobbin and G. Garrett. 2008. "Introduction: The Diffusion of Liberalization." in *The Global Diffusion of Markets and Democracy*, edited by Beth Simmons, Frank Dobbin and Geoffrey Garrett, pp. 1–64. New York, NY: Cambridge University Press.

Skidelsky, R. 2000. *John Maynard Keynes: Fighting for Freedom, 1937–1946*. New York, NY: Penguin.

Skocpol, T. and V. Williamson. 2012. *The Tea Party and the Remaking of Republican Conservatism*. New York, NY: Oxford University Press.

Smith, A. 1986. "State-Making and Nation-Building." in *States in History*, edited by John A. Hall. Oxford: Blackwell.

Smith, M. 1992. *Power, Norms and Inflation*. New York, NY: Aldine de Gruyter.

———. 2013. "Beyond the Comfort Zone: Internal Crisis and External Challenge in the European Union's Response to Rising Powers." *International Affairs* 89(3): 653–671.

Snyder, J. 2000. *From Voting to Violence: Democratization and Nationalist Conflict*. Norton: New York.

Snyder, R. and R. Bhavnani. 2005. "Diamonds, Blood and Taxes: A Revenue-Centred Framework for Explaining Political Order." *Journal of Conflict Resolution* 49(4): 563–597.

Steil, B. 2013. *The Battle of Bretton Woods; John Maynard Keynes, Harry Dexter White and the Making of a New World Order*. Princeton, NJ: Princeton University Press.

Stepan, A., J. Linz and Y. Yadav. 2011. *Crafting State-Nations: India and Other Multinational Democracies*. Baltimore, MD: Johns Hopkins.

Stepan, A. and G. Robertson. 2003. "An 'Arab' More Than a 'Muslim' Electoral Gap." *Journal of Democracy* 14(3): 30–44.

Stiglitz, J. 2012. *The Price of Inequality: How Today's Divided Society Endangers Our Future*. New York, NY: Norton.

Stockolm International Peace Research Institute. 2012. Trends in World Military Expenditure, 2012. Stockholm: SIPRI. http://books.sipri.org/product_info?c_product_id=458# (Accessed January 2013).

Streeck, W. 1997. "German Capitalism: Does It Exist? Can It Survive?" in *Political Economy of Modern Capitalism*, edited by Colin Crouch and Wolfgang Streeck, pp. 33–54. Thousand Oaks, CA: Sage.

L160-L0

L161-L0

L162-L0

L163-L0

L164-L0

L165-L0

L166-L0

L167-L0

L168-L0

L169-L0

L170-L0

L171-L0

L172-L0

L173-L0

L174-L0

L175-L0

L176-L0

L177-L0

L178-L0

L179-L0

L180-L0

L181-L0

L182-L0

L183-L0

L184-L0

L185-L0

L186-L0

L187-L0

L188-L0

L189-L0

L190-L0

L191-L0

L192-L0

L193-L0

L194-L0

L195-L0

L196-L0

L197-L0

L198-L0

L199-L0

L200-L0
L201-L0

———. 2009. *Reforming Capitalism: Institutional Change in the German Political Economy*. New York, NY: Oxford University Press.

Subramanian, A. 2011. *Eclipse: Living in the Shadow of China's Economic Dominance*. Washington, DC: Peterson Institute for International Economics.

Swank, D. 2002. *Global Capital, Political Institutions and Policy Change in Developed Welfare States*. New York, NY: Cambridge University Press.

Teles, S. 2008. *The Rise of the Conservative Legal Movement*. Princeton, NJ: Princeton University Press.

Thelen, K. and I. Kume. 1999. "The Effects of 'Globalization' on Labor Revisited: Lessons from Germany and Japan." *Politics and Society* 27(4): 476–504.

Trentmann, F. 2008. *Free Trade Nation: Consumption, Civil Society and Commerce in Modern Britain*. Oxford: Oxford University Press.

Treverton, G. 1978. *The Dollar Drain and American Forces in Germany: Managing the Political Economics of Alliances*. Columbus: Ohio University Press.

Trigger, B. 2003. *Understanding Early Civilizations: A Comparative Study*. Cambridge: Cambridge University Press.

Tsoukalis, L. 2003. *What Kind of Europe?* Oxford: Oxford University Press.

United Nations Conference on Trade and Development. 2013. *Global Foreign Direct Investment Declined by 18% in 2012, Annual Report Says*. Washington, DC: UNCTAD. http://unctad.org/en/pages/PressRelease.aspx?OriginalVersionID=143 (Accessed January 2014).

U.S. Central Intelligence Agency. 2014. *CIA World Factbook*. https://www.cia.gov/library/publications/the-world-factbook/geos/ci.html (Accessed May 2014).

U.S. Department of Commerce, Bureau of the Census. 1975. *Historical Statistics of the United States*. Washington, DC: U.S. Government Printing Office.

U.S. Department of Defense. 2013. *Base Structure Report, Fiscal Year 2013 Baseline*. Washington, DC: U.S. Department of Defense. http://www.acq.osd.mil/ie/download/bsr/Base%20Structure%20Report%202013_06242013.pdf (Accessed November 2013).

U.S. Federal Reserve. 2013a. *Balance of Current Account, 1960–2013*. St. Louis, Washington, DC: Federal Reserve Bank of St. Louis. http://research.stlouisfed.org/fred2/graph/?id=BOPBCA (Accessed November 2013).

———. 2013b. *Federal Debt: Total Public Debt as Percent of Gross Domestic Product*. St. Louis, Washington, DC: Federal Reserve Bank of St. Louis. http://research.stlouisfed.org/fred2/series/GFDEGDQ188S (Accessed November 2013).

U.S. Office of Management and Budget. 2013. *The President's Budget for Fiscal Year 2014*. Washington, DC: U.S. Office of Management sand Budget. http://www.whitehouse.gov/omb/budget (Accessed November 2013).

U.S. Social Security Administration. 2013. "A Summary of the 2013 Annual Report." http://www.ssa.gov/oact/trsum/ (Accessed November 2013).

Van der Pijl, K. 1984. *The Making of an Atlantic Ruling Class*. London: New Left Books.

Veblen, T. 1915. *Imperial German and the Industrial Revolution*. New York: Macmillan.

Vezirgiannidou, S. 2013. "The United States and Rising Powers in a Post-hegemonic Global Order." *International Affairs* 89(3): 635–651.

Vogel, S. 1996. *Freer Markets, More Rules: Regulatory Reform in Advanced Countries*. Ithaca, NY: Cornell University Press.

Wade, R. and F. Veneroso. 1998a. "The Asian Crisis: The High Debt Model Versus the Wall Street-Treasury-IMF Complex." *New Left Review* 228: 3–24.

———. 1998b. "The Gathering World Slump and the Battle Over Capital Controls." *New Left Review* 231: 13–42.

Weber, M. 1980. *Wirtschaft und Gesellschaft: Grundriss der verstehenden Soziologie*. Tubingen: J.C.B Mohr.

References

Weisman, J. 2014. "Spending Plan Ignores Overhaul for IMF." *The New York Times,* January 16, A14.

Weiss, L. 1998. *The Myth of the Powerless State.* Ithaca, NY: Cornell University Press.

———. 2003. "Guiding Globalization in East Asia: New Roles for Old Developmental States." in *States in the Global Economy,* edited by Linda Weiss, pp. 245–270. New York, NY: Cambridge University Press.

———. 2014. *America Inc.? Innovation and Enterprise in the National Security State.* Ithaca, NY: Cornell University Press.

Western, B. and K. Beckett. 1999. "How Unregulated is the U.S. Labor Market? The Penal System as a Labor Market Institution." *American Journal of Sociology* 104: 1030–1060.

Wilkinson, R. and K. Pickett. 2009. *The Spirit Level: Why Greater Equality Makes Societies Stronger.* New York, NY: Bloomsbury.

Wilson, W.J. 2006. *When Work Disappears.* New York, NY: Knopf.

Wimmer, A. 2013. *Waves of War: Nationalism, State Formation, and Ethnic Exclusion in the Modern World.* Cambridge: Cambridge University Press.

World Bank. 2013a. *Current Account Balance.* Washington, DC: World Bank. http://data.worldbank.org/indicator/BN.CAB.XOKA.CD (Accessed November 2013).

———. 2013b. *GDP Growth (Annual %).* Washington, DC: World Bank. http://data.worldbank.org/indicator/NY.GDP.MKTP.KD.ZG (Accessed December 2013).

———. 2014. *World Data Bank/World Development Indicators.* Washington: World Bank. http://databank.worldbank.org/data/views/reports/tableview.aspx (Accessed March 2014).

World Economic Forum. 2012. *The Global Competitiveness Report, 2012–2013.* Geneva: World Economic Forum.

———. 2013. *The Global Competitiveness Report, 2013–2014.* Geneva: World Economic Forum.

World Trade Organization. 2013. *International Trade Statistics.* Geneva: WTO. http://www.wto.org/english/res_e/statis_e/its2013_e/its13_appendix_e.htm (Accessed December 2013).

Worsley, P. 1984. *The Three Worlds: Culture and Human Development.* London: Weidenfeld and Nicolson.

Worstall, T. 2011. "China Makes Almost Nothing Out of Apple's iPads and iPhones." *Forbes,* December 24. http://www.forbes.com/sites/timworstall/2011/12/24/china-makes-almost-nothing-out-of-apples-ipads-and-i/ (Accessed November 2013).

Zucker, S., C. Deutsch, J. Hoerr, N. Jonas, J. Pearson and J. Cooper. 1982. *The Reindustrialization of America.* New York, NY: McGraw-Hill.

INDEX

Note: The letter "n" following locators refers to notes.

Index

Index

Hitler, Adolf 22, 115
Hobbes, Thomas 1–2, 3, 14
Holocaust 4
Home Rule 19
homogeneity 4, 17, 45, 53, 70, 116–17
Hong Kong 53, 116
Hopewell, Kristen 48
Huguenots 15
Hull, Cordell 22
human capital 15, 31, 36, 37, 48–9
human rights 54
Hungary 23
Huntington, Samuel 75
Hyundai 45

IMF, *see* International Monetary Fund (IMF)
imitation 13–14
immigration 48–9
imperialism: in Africa 20, 66, 67
    British Empire 18–20, 26–7, 41
    collapse of empires 11
    decolonization 30–1, 34, 65
    definition of empires 10
    and ethnic identity 66
    and France 30–1
    impact on weak states 65–6
    Imperial China 11, 12, 13
    and nationalism 17–21, 22, 24, 69–70
    pre-industrial 10–12
    Roman Empire 11–12
    and the United States 40–1
inclusion 2, 3, 16–17
India 56–9
    corruption in 51, 58
    democracy in 46, 56
    economy of 50, 57
    embedded autonomy in 39, 58
    geopolitical role of 58–9
    languages in 56–7, 116
    liberal reforms in 57–8
    as a multinational nation-state 4, 16
    national identity in 116
    nationalism in 57, 61
    nuclear weapons in 58
    as part of the British Empire 20
    relations with China 57, 58, 61
    relations with Pakistan 36–7, 58, 61
    relations with the Soviet Union 58
    role of the state in 61
    Tata Steel 34
    see also BRICs
Indonesia 7, 33, 35, 64, 71, 74, 75–6
Industrial and Commercial Bank 34
inequality: in Brazil 59
    in Chile 76
    in China 50, 54–5

in South Africa 72
    in the United States 112–13
inflation 32, 95n. 51
information technology 32
Institutional Revolutionary Party (PRI) 77
institution building 24
institutions 3, 5, 8, 33, 38, 48, 63, 70–1, 85
International Atomic Energy Agency 58
International Monetary Fund (IMF) 27, 33, 35, 38,
    48, 54, 110, 114, 117
Iran 36, 37, 40, 52, 71, 103
Iraq 36, 64
Iraq War 38, 93, 95, 96, 101, 102, 102n. 11, 103
Ireland 19, 85, 88
Islam 74, 75–6
Ismay, Lord 25
Israel 37, 40
Italy 10, 25, 82, *see also* Roman Empire

Japan: and currency issues 32, 110
    economic power of 33, 43, 79
    inequality in 112
    loss of power 99
    manufacturing in 104
    relations with China 54, 61, 106
    relations with South Korea 45
    role of the state in 39
    statism in 80, 81, 84
    and United States 13, 37
    war with Russia 17
    in World War II 22
Johnson, Lyndon 95
Joseph, Franz 15

Kazakhstan 37, 52
Kennedy, Paul 99
Keynes, John Maynard 27, 28, 34–5, 118
Khaldun, Ibn 12
Khrushchev, Nikita 29
kidnappings 73
Kissinger, Henry 29
Kosovo 96
Kurds 74–5
Kuwait 33

labor movements 26, 107n. 25
labor relations 84
Lagarde, Christine 110
Lange, Matthew 37
languages: in the European Union 89, 116
    in India 56–7, 116
    used in education 43–4
law and economics approach 108
liberalism: in Britain 16–17
    and capitalism 79–80, 82
    classical 2

Index

Obama, Barack 111, 118
oil 31, 39–40, 73, 103
O'Neill, Eugene 29
order 2, 3, 5, 7, 9, 63, 79, 99, 115
Organization of African States 67
Organization of Petroleum Exporting Countries
    (OPEC) 40
outsourcing 32, 78

Pakistan 36–7, 58, 61, 64n. 5, 65, 71, 73
Palacký, František 18
Parsons, Talcott 12
performance of state power 12
Perry, William 95
Peru 77
Philippines 71
Pinochet, Augusto 35, 76
pluralism 91–2
Poland 23, 93
population transfer 4, 23
Portugal 82
Posner, Richard 108
postwar era 6, 9, 23–8, 95, 103
poverty 50, 55, 68, *see also* inequality
power: balance of 3, 8
    and capitalism 32–4
    centralization of 45–6
    inequality of 38
    and international institutions 38
    loss of 99
    state power 1, 3, 9, 12, 115
    of the United States 6, 8, 32–4, 38–41,
        99–114
Princip, Gavrilo 20
protection, *see* security
protectionism 22, 114
Proust, Marcel 93
Putin, Vladimir 36, 51, 52, 94

Qatar 33, 37, 64n. 5

race 108, 112
radicalism 2, 16–17, 66
Reagan, Ronald 107, 117, 118
realism 14
Roman Empire 11–12
Roosevelt, Franklin D. 34–5
Rousseau, Jean-Jacques 14
Russia 7, 51–2
    agriculture in 45–6
    economic characteristics of 50, 51–2
    Gazprom 34
    geopolitical role of 36, 52, 94
    life expectancy in 51
    military characteristics of 50, 52

and national identity 52
and nationalism 17–18, 61
neoliberalism in 117
role of the state in 61
and Syria 117
war with Japan 17
in World War I 22
    see also BRICs; Soviet Union
Rwanda 30, 66, 68

SABIC 34
Salisbury, Lord 20
Samsung 45
Samuels, Richard 39
Sanderson, Thomas 117
Sartre, Jean-Paul 16, 100
Saudi Arabia 32, 33, 34, 103
Schumpeter, Joseph 103
Scott, James 45
secession 4, 18
security 2, 3, 5, 7, 9, 63, 99, 115
Seeley, John 19
seigniorage, *see* currency issues
self-interest 100
sense of belonging, *see* belonging, sense of
Shaw, George Bernard 4
Sierra Leone 65, 68
Singapore 31, 33, 39
Single European Act 86
size 6, 8, 9, 17, 120
Smith, Adam 13, 15, 40
Smith, Michael 88
Snowden, Edward 102–3
social democracy 83
social engineering 74, 75
socialism 16–17
Somalia 7, 64, 66
Sombart, Werner 6, 21
South Africa 34, 64, 69, 71–3, 74
South East Asian Treaty Organization (SEATO)
    102
South Korea 33, 39, 44–5, 54, 71
Soviet Union: collapse of 34–5, 46, 65, 107
    nationalism in 23
    and nuclear weapons 29
    postwar era in 23
    relations with India 58
    sense of belonging in 23
    as a threat 47
    see also Russia
Spain 14, 31, 77, 82, 90
Sri Lanka 37, 116
stagflation 35, 40
Stalin, Joseph 23, 115
Standard Bank Group 34

Index

impact of imperialism 65–6
intervention in 70
measurement of 63–4
poverty in 68
role of institutions 70–1
state capacity in 1, 5–6, 115
taxation in 67
Weber, Max 4–5, 11, 16, 17, 20, 21
welfare state 14, 24, 26, 55, 81
When Things Fell Apart (Bates) 68
White, Henry Dexter 27
Wilhelm II 20, 21
Wolfowitz, Paul 103
World Bank 27, 33, 38, 54, 117

World Economic Forum (WEF) 31, 110
World Trade Organization (WTO) 27, 33, 48, 54, 58, 59
World War I 20–2
World War II 22
postwar era 6, 9, 23–8, 95, 103
WTO, *see* World Trade Organization (WTO)

Yudhoyono, Susilo Bambang 74

Zaire, *see* Democratic Republic of Congo
Zambia 71
Zimbabwe 64, 68, 69
Zuma, Jacob 72